KT-218-052

AMAZON ORIGINAL

The Grand Tour

GUIDE TO THE WORLD*

* some of it at least

WARNING Some of this book is factual but most of it isn't. Many of the observations are incorrect and the advice idiotic. *The Grand Tour* accepts no responsibility for anything that happens to you as a result of following tips or imitating actions you read about in these pages. Basically, it's your fault if you get thrown out of the first-class lounge/an aeroplane/France.

HarperCollins*Publishers*
1 London Bridge Street
London SE1 9GF

www.harpercollins.co.uk

First published by HarperCollins*Publishers* 2017

10 9 8 7 6 5 4 3 2 1

© W. Chump & Sons Limited 2017

Illustrations on pp 4–5, 7, 8, 9, 16, 18, 26, 30, 36, 38, 39, 44, 50, 62, 72, 84, 92, 102, 104, 105, 106, 112, 118, 122, 124, 130, 142, 144, 154, 155, 156, 162, 164, 168, 170, 172, 174, 176, 178, 184, 186, 188, 189, 198, 200, 206, 210, 211, 212, 216, 225, 230, 232, 238, 240, 272 © Jenni Sparks

The author asserts the moral right to be identified as the author of this work

While every effort has been made to trace the owners of copyright material reproduced herein and secure permissions, the publishers would like to apologise for any omissions and will be pleased to incorporate missing acknowledgements in any future edition of this book.

A catalogue record of this book is available from the British Library

ISBN 978-0-00-825785-9

Printed and bound at GPS Group

All rights reserved. No part of this publication may be reproduced, stored in a retrieval system, or transmitted, in any form or by any means, electronic, mechanical, photocopying, recording or otherwise, without the prior written permission of the publishers.

This book is produced from independently certified FSC™ paper to ensure responsible forest management.

For more information visit: www.harpercollins.co.uk/green

AMAZON ORIGINAL

The Grand Tour

GUIDE TO THE WORLD

HarperCollins*Publishers*

CONTENTS

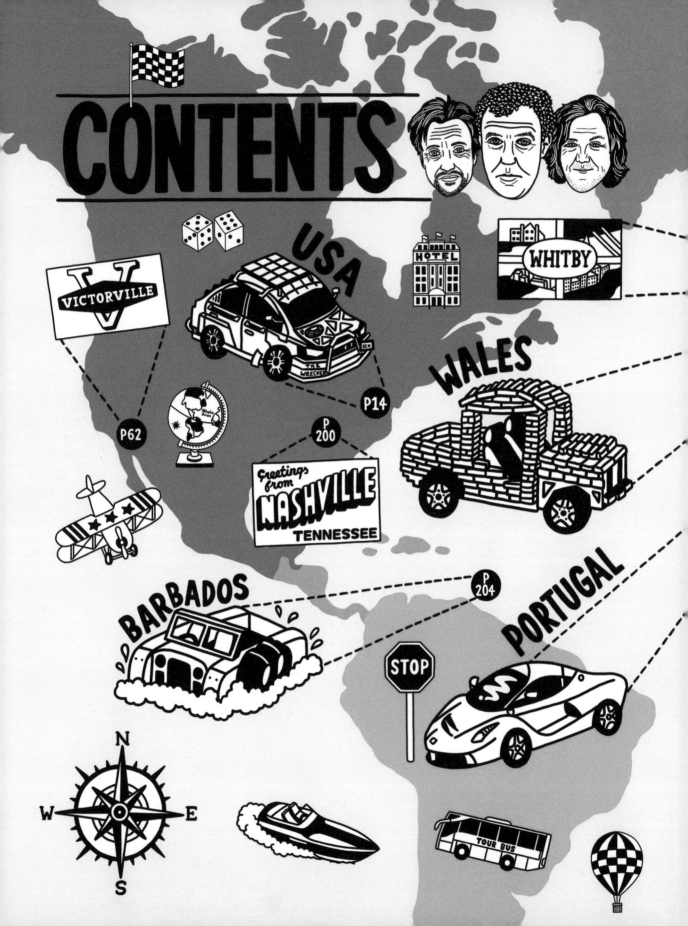

USA

VICTORVILLE

THE WRECKER

HOTEL

WHITBY

WALES

Greetings from NASHVILLE TENNESSEE

BARBADOS

PORTUGAL

STOP

TOUR BUS

N W E S

People often say, 'It's a small world.' But if you asked them to walk from Berlin to Cape Town they'd probably make a huge fuss and insist on taking an aeroplane. That's because the world is, in fact, massive. It can also seem a strange and daunting place, but not if you have the right guide. And that's where we come in. No one is more seasoned at crossing the world than *The Grand Tour*. No one has been through more airports, stayed in more hotels, spoken to more local people and learned more indigenous words for 'sorry about this'. That's why *The Grand Tour* is uniquely placed to show you around some of the high spots of this huge world of ours and to share with you our wisdom, our skills and our holiday photographs. This book is not just an indispensable guide. In fact, it's not an indispensable guide at all. A lot of the information in it is wrong and possibly dangerous. We're not sure. Even so, whenever you're travelling, be certain to keep this book close to you – and as long as you only look at the pictures you should be fine. Remember, it's a big world out there, and we're all somewhere in it. Except astronauts.

CLARKSON, HAMMOND & MAY

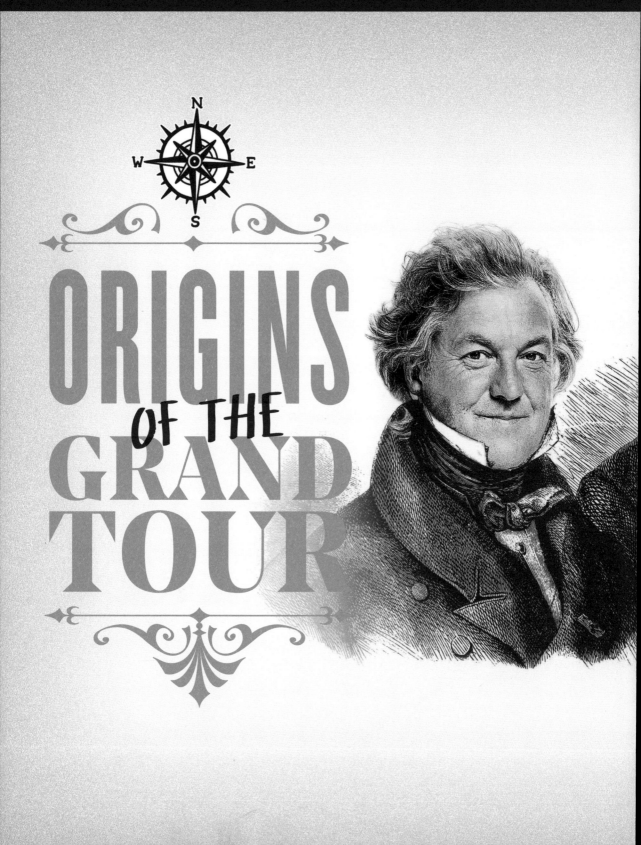

ORIGINS
OF THE
GRAND
TOUR

Originally, a Grand Tour was a 17th- to 19th-century pursuit in which, say, three chums would find themselves at a loose end for whatever reason and would agree to travel together to foreign lands for the purposes of cultural and spiritual enrichment, and also to find out if the Aston Martin DB11 was any good. Before departing one of the friends might say, 'Look, this isn't completely convenient for me. I'm supposed to be making a Christmas special about 1970s toys,' and the other two would reply, 'Oh for God's sake, James. How long does that take? Get a bloody move on,' and then the two idle friends would wait for a bit, and then for a bit longer while their third friend spent a week packing his clothes very neatly into a leather suitcase, and then they would away on their travels.

WHAT DO YOU MEAN, YOU'RE OFF TO MAKE A PROGRAMME ABOUT PUTTING THINGS BACK TOGETHER?

Their destinations might be many and varied, often inspired by a map on the wall of their new office in the Chiswick area of London, which they would look at until they found somewhere that sounded interesting, perhaps having checked what was to be found there using an information source such as *The Encyclopaedia Wikipedia*. Having established that somewhere was interesting, the chums would set off and before you knew it they would find themselves in Italy, where they would attend displays of local art and sculpture and visit the opera, apart from one of

FOR HE
DID MANIE
POWRE
SLYDES

the friends who would perhaps behave like the kind of total moron who thinks *Così fan tutte* is ice cream.

Perhaps soon after, the chums would find themselves in the north of France, which is very underrated actually, especially if you like drizzle, and here one of the friends might devote his time to visiting a local adult souvenirs emporium, where he would purchase a very rude item for the purposes of making an unhelpful directional aid for one of his colleagues while ignoring the gentleman behind the counter who was saying the French for, 'Ah, hello, sir. It's been a while since we've seen you in here.'

After this, the friends' Grand Tour adventure of learning and enrichment and dicking about might take them to Morocco, where the noisiest of the friends would not shut up about terrible Italian things, or they might move on to the exotic climes of the Caribbean to do something that didn't seem especially relevant, or they might even find themselves in Jordan, where they would challenge themselves and would say to themselves only a long time afterwards, 'Oh heavens, this hasn't gone down very well at home.'

The purpose of the Grand Tour was not only to educate and inform, it was also to generate entertainment, ideally about 12 to 13 hours of it. Having achieved this in a single year, the friends might then agree to do it again the following year but in different places, and perhaps the slow, slightly boring one would say, 'I'd like to be the fast one who shouts for a change,' and his friends would say, 'Shhh, James. Don't spoil it.'

PIT STOP 01
USA

FOCUS ON CALIFORNIA

CANADA
(LIKE THE USA, BUT MORE
SOFTLY SPOKEN)

VICTORVILLE

UNITED
STATES OF
AMERICA
(BIG PLACE, LIKES CHEESE)

HOTEL

SOUTH
AMERICA
(LIKE NORTH AMERICA, BUT SPICIER)

a.k.a.
GOLDEN STATE

Former Governors of California include Ronald Reagan and Arnold Schwarzenegger. By 2022, Californians expect to welcome Governor Kardashian.

Population:
39 MILLION

If California were a country, it would have the sixth-largest economy in the world. If California were a country it would also, like, ohmyGurrrd, have way cooler bank notes and stuff.

THE OFFICIAL STATE SLOGAN IS, 'OH, LIKE, WOW, HAVE YOU LOST WEIGHT?'

California produces most of America's peaches, dates, avocados and insincerity.

Currency:
US DOLLAR

California has been immortalised in film many times with movies such as *L.A. Story*, *L.A. Confidential*, *Beverly Hills Cop* and *Miss Marple Goes to Compton*.

Famous people:
EVERYONE

Northern California is home to Silicon Valley whereas Southern California is home to silicon mountains.

Capital:
SACRAMENTO. NOT LA. DON'T SAY LA. IT'S NOT LA. OR SAN FRANCISCO.

BEHIND THE SCENES

Hundreds of cars, thousands of people, a legendary band, and three old men in shirts. That's what made up the big opening for the first series of *The Grand Tour*. Oh, and months and months of planning. Sometimes, even this show plans stuff.

The Breitling Jet Team making one of three passes over the stage. Looked simple, actually required the main road in the background to be closed. To the right, this is James's 'Ooh, I've seen a plane' face.

Below, the specially made sign of fire for what Jeremy christened the 'Burning Van' festival. Because what you need in the desert are more hot things.

Yes, that's a Merlin aircraft engine in a vintage Rolls-Royce. As you can see, it's pure May bait.

Looks like a hellish vision from an apocalyptic near-future. Actually built by a bunch of bright, articulate and super-polite engineers. So maybe the apocalyptic future won't be so bad.

Above, the audience get excited. Apart from that bloke with the beard and sunglasses. Below, before filming starts, Jeremy gets inexorably drawn towards a man with a massive V8.

A rat-rod truck behind a fleet of new cars. The up-to-date stuff was sourced direct from manufacturers.

Our triumphant trio get up on stage in front of the crowd for the first time. An insults contest broke out shortly afterwards, much of which had to be edited out of the final show.

Left, a dragon with a petrol engine. Obviously. Much of this stuff usually stars at the Burning Man festival.

Clarkson spots *The Grand Tour* photographer, May does some light flamenco.

LESSER-KNOWN SONGS ABOUT

CALIFORNIA

CALIFORNIA REPUBLIC

The Golden State has inspired a great many musicians over the years. Here are some California-themed songs that you might not have heard of.

THE GRANDEST OF OPENINGS

IN JEREMY'S HEAD (PHONES)

The very first sequence of *The Grand Tour* episode 1 might well be one of the most enormous opening scenes ever attempted by a television show.

Yet the origins of this massive spectacle came from a very small place, which was the music player on Jeremy's phone. Normally this is a dark and unsettling place full of rock dinosaurs and 19-hour flute solos but in this case it yielded gold.

Clarkson had been wrestling with how we should announce the arrival of the new show until the moment he clicked upon Hothouse Flowers' version of 'I Can See Clearly Now'. From there the whole narrative – leaving London in the rain, arriving in sunny LA to a bright new beginning, a drive through the desert, the gathering up of a huge flotilla of vehicles, the arrival at a massive cars and music festival – flowed from his mind, as a fully formed and inspired thought. Having a thought is one thing, however. Making it all a reality wasn't so easy. Organising all the cars that would make up the amazing Mad Max cavalcade took several months of work inside a 'war room' at GT HQ in London, its walls covered in pictures, maps and diagrams. And it wasn't just the cars themselves; it was finding people who could drive them, and who could be schooled in the discipline of holding position while camera cars and filming helicopters swirled around them in a thick pall of dust.

The presenters themselves would be in a trio of supercars, starting with Jeremy in the new Ford GT. But when that car wasn't available in time the team hatched a plan B involving three tuned Mustangs. Well, we were in America.

Then there was finding a desert location for the 'festival'. A suitable spot was found and all the relevant permissions granted, only for it to become clear that even this vast tract of land wasn't big enough to secure decent shots of the entire flotilla blasting across the landscape. So what you see in the final cut is the convoy driving across two different desert locations, stitched together by TV magic so that they appear seamlessly to pull up to the stage and the crowd around it.

Getting the timing right for this last segment wasn't easy either. In one smooth movement the convoy had to come to a halt while Jeremy, Richard and James continued through the crowd in their Mustangs, got out and walked up onto the stage just as Hothouse Flowers wrapped up their song. Get it wrong, and the whole sequence would need a time-consuming re-set of cars, cameras and people.

To add another layer to the mix, the show got wind that the Breitling Jet Display team were at an air show down the road and asked if they'd mind popping over for a fly-past. Or rather three fly-pasts, since this gave more opportunities to get the shots.

Over 200 people were involved in the filming of that day, not including the vast and heroically upbeat audience who stood in the heat all afternoon, whooping and cheering long after their voices had gone hoarse.

Thankfully everything went to plan and the sequence played out just as it had appeared in Jeremy's head, back when he first randomly found an old song on his phone.

TITLE SEQUENCE
CAR LIST

When planning the massive opening sequence for the start of a brand new television show, it's important to have certain things. An epic desert location. A stage upon which a band can perform a classic and catchy song. A fast Mustang for each of your presenters. But it's also a good idea to have other cars. Lots of other cars. Lots and lots of other cars. So that's what we did. These are they.

Alfa Romeo 4C, Arctic Cat Wildcat X, Ariel Nomad, Aston Martin V8 Vantage S, Audi R8, Baja Jeep, Bentley Continental GT V8 S, BMW i8, BMW M5, Cadillac CTS-V, Cadillac CT6 , Class I Baja buggy, Dodge Challenger Hellcat, Ford F-150 Raptor, Ford F-150 sand rail, Ford F-450, Ford Focus RS, Ford Ranger off-road truck, Freightliner Pikes Peak, Jaguar F-Type SVR, Jeep Crew Chief 715, Jeep FC-150, Lamborghini Aventador SV, Lotus Elise, Mazda Miata Super20, Mercedes-AMG GT S, Mercedes G65 AMG, Mitsubishi Evo X Battlecar, Morgan 3-wheeler, Morgan Roadster, Need for Speed Porsche 911 Widebody, Nissan GT-R, Porsche 911 Carrera, Rolls-Royce Ascot Tourer, Vuhl 05, and the off-road Dodge Charger, Fast Attack Buggy and Plymouth Road Runner from the *Fast & Furious* movies. In case you're interested, the presenters' cars were: Jeremy: Galpin Fisker Ford Mustang Rocket; Richard: Ford Mustang Shelby GT350R; James: Roush Stage 3 Mustang. Oh, and the planes were Aero L-39C Albatrosses flown by the Breitling Jet Team.

3 MINUTES WITH ...

JEREMY CLARKSON

**A rapid-fire Q&A with the former
local newspaper journalist turned
Grand Tour presenter**

> **MAY IS A THIEF, A COMMON THIEF**

HELLO, JEREMY.

Yes, yes, yes, hello. Have you seen my reading glasses?

Aren't they –

This is literally the millionth pair I've lost. Where do they all go? It's James, isn't it. James is stealing them. He's a thief, you know.

But I think they're –

It's literally impossible for any human being to keep a pair of glasses for more than 10 seconds and I've realised this is literally all the fault of James May.

They're on your head.

Most things in life are, when you get down to it, the fault of James May. War, pestilence, disease, being unable to find the place where they keep the teaspoons in someone else's kitchen – all May's fault in some way or other that we've yet to fathom. I know I'm right on this one.

Yes, but in this case your reading glasses are on your head.

What?

They're on your head.

Yes, I knew that.

So, first question...

Yes, he is.

What?

Yes, he is. James May. Is he a thief? Yes, he is. I assume that was going to be your first question. Is James May...

Um, Richard Hammond...

What? Is James May Richard Hammond? What a stupid question. Did you go to journalism college?

No, the first question was going to be, 'Richard Hammond: can you describe him in three words?'

Can they be swear words?

Not really.

No.

I'm sorry?

My answer is no. Can I describe Richard Hammond in three words? If they can't be swear words then, no, I can't. Literally impossible.

Oh. What about James May?

No, I imagine he wouldn't be able to either.

No, I mean, can you describe James Ma-
Oh for God's sake, where are my glasses?

You've put them back on your hea-
May! MAY!

Jeremy leaves the room. From the office next door there is some shouting. Jeremy returns to the room.

He says he hasn't taken them, but I know he has. A thief. A common thief, that's what he is. Right, what were you saying?

Well...

From outside there is a protracted clattering sound.

What was that?
Don't worry, it was probably just Hammond falling down the stairs.

Falling down the stairs?
Yes, he does it all the time. Nothing to worry about.

Are you sure?
No, but I can't be bothered to get up again.

Oh, okay. Um, shall we get back to the questions?
Okay, to answer your question, yes, Richard Hammond is a type of swear word. At least, he is in this room. I'll give you an example of what Richard Hammond means in this room: 'Oh no, I've just stepped in a Hammond.' By which I mean, 'dog turd'.

Why would there be a dog turd in this room?
An actual dog turd, or Richard Hammond?

No, I ... never mind. Next question, can you sum up *The Grand Tour* in three words?
Yes. 'The'. 'Grand'. And 'Tour'. It's already three words. You're really not paying attention, are you?

Well, it was more of an abstract question.
I literally don't know what you mean. Literally. You're just wasting time.

Speaking of which, I think our time is up.
Good, because I need to find my glasses. I put them somewhere safe.

They're on your head.
Yes, I know. Now please go away.

MOTORING FACTS
FROM AROUND

IN ITALY A DRIVER MUST KEEP AT LEAST ONE HAND ON THE WHEEL AT ALL TIMES, <u>UNLESS EATING A HOT MEAL.</u>

In Senegal you must have a hat in your car at all times, although not for the normal reasons.

In Uzbekistan it is illegal to run over your mother, unless it is a weekday.

THE WORLD

100% **FALSE** AT TIME OF PRINT

SHOUTING!

If you stop at a T-junction in northern Sweden you must remember to shout 'BRONCO!' out of your car window.

When driving in New Zealand, don't forget your Car Jennifer. If you don't know what a Car Jennifer is, ask a Police Peter.

In the Chinese province of Ped Xing it is illegal to touch the steering wheel.

In Norway every extra horsepower over 100 is taxed at a rate of two horsepower. As a consequence, the Norwegian-market Ferrari 488 has minus 1100 horsepower.

TAXI !!!!

The actor Daniel Day-Lewis always encounters problems when visiting Indonesia as his name literally translates as 'Call me a taxi'.

The South African driving test is the only one in the world that contains a section on fighting off an attacker.

If taking your driving test in Chile, don't forget your Driving Owl, which should be relatively clean and presented without hesitation or wiping.

MOTORING FACTS FROM AROUND

The oldest person ever to pass their driving test was Hector Esposito of Monclova, Mexico, who was awarded his licence at the age of 103. Four years later he was disqualified from driving after a routine police stop discovered him to be dead.

In Tonga the king has not heard of cars and as a result everyone else must pretend they have not heard of cars either, even though they have.

In 1976 Sweden passed a new law stating that all motorists must throw a fresh fish out of their car window at 1km intervals. The law was repealed eight months later when it was discovered that the country had accidentally elected a herring gull as prime minister.

In Malaysia the penalty for being caught speeding is that you must eat your entire car, even the hot bits.

In Finland the driving test includes a requirement for new motorists to 'prove they can hover in a stable way'. That's because the Finnish word for 'car' is the same as the Finnish word for 'enormous helicopter' and the government can't be bothered to sort it out.

In Arkansas it is illegal to drive with your eyes shut, unless it's raining.

THE WORLD

IN COLOMBIA IT IS ILLEGAL FOR A GOAT TO DRIVE A CAR, <u>UNLESS IT HAS PASSED ITS DRIVING TEST</u>.

WILLYS

WHJ 043
CIRCASIA

WILLYS

For most people Ford Escort is a car, but not for the people of Uruguay who, in 1987, elected a man called Ford Escort as their president. His first act was to ban the sale of the Ford Escort in his country on the grounds that it was 'confusing'.

In Japan denting another car is punishable by feeling very embarrassed for up to three years.

POSTCARD

FROM THE TENT

JOHANNESBURG

Came to Johannesburg to record the first show in the series, even though it'll be the second to go live. That way if it all goes wrong, we've got more time to fix it.

First time we'd seen the tent put up since we gave it a trial run on a damp farm in Hertfordshire a few months ago. Looks a bit better here. First night, sent James off to go spinning. He came back to the hotel bar covered in dirt and stinking like a tyre fire. Decided having a beer was more important than getting changed, even though bar was packed. Maybe people think he always smells like that. Lion costume delivered, to 'eat' a star guest. It's been hard to find a realistic one. Ignored Jeremy's suggestion to 'use a real lion'. Next day

we filmed the show. Presenters liked the idea of first studio recording being here because they've performed live shows in South Africa before and the audiences are always amazing which makes everything go with a swing. Sure enough, they were great. Everyone on the crew happy, had a small party back at the hotel at which Richard bought half the bar and Jeremy made our Dutch tech team race around the hotel garden. Up late this morning, about to go to airport then remembered we needed to make short film for very important American TV critics' conference apologising for not being there. Remembered animal costume used yesterday so got one of crew to put it on and deliver message to camera as a talking lion while presenters sat in the background. American TV critics will think we're a bit strange. Oh well. See you soon,

THE GRAND TOUR

MOTORCYCLE STUNTMAN

RICHEVEL KHAMMONDEVEL

SEE HIM FALL FROM HIS MOTORCYCLE

WATCH HIM GET BACK ON AGAIN

SEE HIM FALL OFF AGAIN

- CARRIES ON EVEN THOUGH HIS FINGER IS A BIT HURTY! -

MULTIPLE FALLS! IS HE OKAY? YES! UNLESS YOU ARE A NEWSPAPER, IN WHICH CASE, ALSO YES! BUT WITH A MORE DRAMATIC HEADLINE!

YOU WON'T BE BOTHERED TO BELIEVE YOUR EYES!

Richevel Khammondevel

PIT STOP 02

PORTUGAL

FOCUS ON PORTUGAL

EUROPE
(OR AT LEAST SOME OF IT)

PORTUGAL (QUITE NARROW)

NORTH AFRICA
LAND OF CONTRASTS. AND SAND.

a.k.a.

REPÚBLICA PORTUGUESA

(if you are Portuguese and also very formal)

Portuguese inventions include peri-peri sauce and therefore also the invention of teenagers going on crap dates to chicken restaurants.

Population:

11 MILLION

The Algarve International Circuit at Portimão is famed for its challenging, technical design, which has been known to make Jeremy Clarkson's house explode.

Capital:

LISBON

THE MOTTO OF PORTUGAL IS 'MMM, CUSTARD TARTS'.

In 1373 Britain and Portugal signed the Anglo-Portuguese Alliance, which is still in force today. This agreement promises that each nation shall defend the other in the event of war, as long as they're not too busy and it's not a bank holiday or anything.

Currency:

EURO

Portuguese explorer Pedro Álvares Cabral was the first European to discover Brazil, although he also found it was too big to bring home with him.

Famous people:

CRISTIANO RONALDO (FOOTBALLER), LUÍS FIGO (FOOTBALLER), RUI COSTA (FOOTBALLER), JOSÉ MOURINHO (FOOTBALL MANAGER), VASCO DA GAMA (NOTHING TO DO WITH FOOTBALL)

From the sixth until the eighth century, the Iberian peninsula was under the control of the Visigoths, who really liked both The Cure and wearing reflective bands on their black clothes if cycling at night.

BEHIND THE SCENES

Before *The Grand Tour* had a name or indeed any other ideas, there was this. A trip to Portugal for the ultimate hypercar shoot-out. That's why no one in this film mentions the name of the show. At that point, it didn't have one. Although James suggested 'Nigel'.

Richard experiences a moment of severe underpant damage at the wheel of the insane P1.

Setting up this shoot took many, many months, not least because McLaren and Ferrari were very particular about the location, the back-up provided and the tyres the cars used. Porsche, less so.

Something we might never see again: James May powersliding. Oh, also, three hypercars together.

The location for this test was the Algarve International Circuit in Portimao. It opened in 2008 and is sometimes used for Formula One testing.

PORTUGAL LAND OF INADVISABLE BETs

'IF THE MCLAREN P1 ISN'T
FASTER THAN THOSE
OTHER TWO CARS YOU
CAN KNOCK MY HOUSE
DOWN ... OH BUGGER'
-JEREMY CLARKSON

'IF THERE'S SUCH A THING
AS MALARIA YOU CAN HAVE
MY VICEROYSHIP OF
PORTUGUESE INDIA
... OH BUGGER'
- VASCO DA GAMA

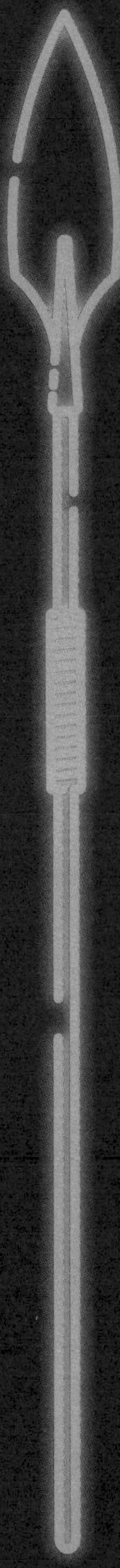

'IF WE DON'T BEAT THESE NORWEGIANS IN THIS CHAMPIONS LEAGUE MATCH I WILL STOP MANAGING CHELSEA (BUT THEN COME BACK AGAIN IN 2013) ... OH BUGGER'

– JOSÉ MOURINHO

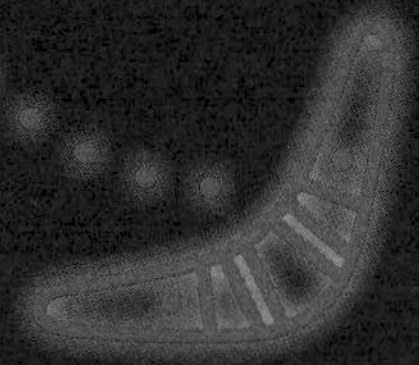

'THERE'S NO WAY THIS SPICY CHICKEN RECIPE IS GOING TO WORK AND IF IT DOES YOU CAN LET A SOUTH AFRICAN MAN USE IT TO BUILD A SUCCESSFUL RESTAURANT CHAIN ... OH BUGGER'

– EVERYONE IN PORTUGAL

'I PROMISE YOU LAPU-LAPU WILL WANT TO CONVERT TO CHRISTIANITY AND IF I'M WRONG YOU CAN STAB ME WITH A BAMBOO SPEAR ... OH BUGGER'

FERDINAND MAGELLAN

GO AWAY MAY

When planning your next holiday, why not consider the advantages of GO AWAY MAY, the only holiday company owned and operated by that James May man who is sometimes on your television.

A holiday from GO AWAY MAY takes away all your normal stresses and replaces them with new stresses, such as the kind brought on by realising that your flight home leaves in 20 minutes and you are still on a coach driven by a shaggy-haired gentleman who believes this is the correct direction despite the exhortations of the other passengers and the local man we ran over a few miles back.

But that's all to come. A GO AWAY MAY holiday starts from the moment you leave your house and have to stand outside it for 47 minutes because your taxi driver is James May and he's had to go back to get your tickets, which he forgot when he left his office.

Once aboard your aeroplane you really can relax, knowing that up in the cockpit the controls are being smoothly operated by James May, who is a fully qualified pilot AND knows the names of two other airports, though neither is where you're supposed to be going.

Finally, you reach your destination hotel, usually within two or three days of the stated arrival time. As you wait for news of the other people in your party, you can sit back in a brown corduroy chair, sip on a pint of bitter and reflect on how the relevant authorities will probably find them soon.

Then it's time to check in to your room, personally organised by James May and containing everything he himself would look for in a hotel, by which we mean two bottles of warm ginger beer and a massive switch that turns all the lights off at once.

As evening falls it's time to visit the restaurant, where you can peruse a high-quality menu knowing that James May has curated the selection personally and that, as a result, it's just a single piece of cardboard with two kinds of pie written on it.

Your holiday starts here. Where it ends, no one knows. James has lost the bit of paper with your details on it.

SAMPLE ACTIVITIES ON YOUR GO AWAY MAY HOLIDAY

The Lazenby-Ruddock transmission overdrive system. A brief guide.
(Running time: 9 hours)

Stripping, inspecting, cleaning and rebuilding a Thrubson 8J-80 carburettor.
(Running time: 14 hours)

Radial-engined aircraft of the inter-war years. A brief history.
(Running time: 19 hours and 2 days)

THE GREATEST CAR-MAKING COUNTRIES ON EARTH

USA

Current annual production: 12 million

Epicentre: Detroit

Most famous cars: Ford Model T, Ford Mustang, Chevrolet Corvette, Ford Thunderbird, and lots of others

Best current model: Ford GT

The USA has two solid claims to being the greatest car-making nation in history, the first being that mass production of cars was perfected here. The second is that, from the Model T to the Mustang, it's made so much memorable stuff. Detroit's best days might be behind it, but the old town rose from the dead after the financial crash and isn't done for yet, even if a lot of the assembly of stuff in the USA now happens under foreign ownership in un-car-y places like Tennessee and Alabama. Even so, the fact remains that America still builds and buys a lot of cars. And some of them are even quite good.

GREAT BRITAIN

Current annual production: 1.8 million

Epicentre: Birmingham

Most famous cars: Mini, Jaguar E-Type, Range Rover, Morris Minor, Jaguar XJ6, and so on.

Best current model: Range Rover

Great Britain was once the world's second-largest car-making nation after the USA and once boasted the world's largest factory, the Austin plant at Longbridge in Birmingham. Britain came up with ground-breaking new models like the Mini, which showed that front-wheel-drive was the way to make a small car, and the Range Rover, which showed that 4x4s weren't just for farmers. But that was all a long time ago. What does Britain have now? Well, it's got over 30 factories, from the vast mass production of Nissan in Sunderland to the gentler pace of tiny companies like Ariel in Somerset, and they're making more cars now than they have in two decades, from the Mini and Honda Civic to the Morgan Three-wheeler and McLaren 720S. When it comes to designing, developing and building cars, Britain is still officially 'quite busy'. And 'quite good'. Any more would lack British understatement.

ITALY

Current annual production: 1.1 million

Epicentre: Turin

Most famous cars: Ferrari 250 GTO, Lamborghini Miura, Alfa Romeo Spider, Fiat 500, Lancia Fulvia, and so on.

Best current model: Ferrari 488 GTB (or, if you ask Jeremy, the Alfa Giulia Quadrifoglio)

What can you say about a country that has given us Ferrari, Lamborghini, Maserati, Alfa Romeo and Lancia? You can say, 'Wait, that sounds like you're describing Italy. They're really good at making sporty cars, aren't they?' Yes. Yes they are. In fact, Italy is historically so good at making fast, beautiful cars crammed with an indefinable

and heady personality that there's a whole book to be written just containing Italian car clichés. They're also, you might note, very good at small cars too. Well, Fiat is. Funnily enough, Ferrari has never tried. You might think that Italy's best days are behind it, but the sensational modern Ferrari range, the wonders of the Alfa Giulia, even the ongoing appeal of the Fiat 500 to anyone who lives in a city and is, or knows someone, called Emma, demonstrates that Italy has still got the skills to pay the bills. And Chrysler's bills too.

FRANCE

Current annual production: 2 million

Epicentre: Paris

Most famous cars: Citroën Traction Avant, Citroën 2CV, Renault 4, Renault 5, Peugeot 205, Citroën DS, etc

Best current model: Alpine A110

You can't leave the French off any list of great car-making nations. They invented the idea of incredibly relaxing cars with suspension so soft the ash wouldn't fall off the end of your untipped cigarette. They invented the practical, swivel-seated people carrier (as long as you forget that the Renault Espace was actually designed in Coventry). They even invented the hot hatchback with the Simca 1100Ti, let VW nab the idea for the Golf GTI, then took it back and used it to smack the Germans in the chops with sensational tearaways like the Peugeot 205 GTi, the Renault 5 GT Turbo, the Citroën AX GT, the Peugeot 306 GTi, the Citroën Saxo VTS, the Renault Clio Williams, the… You get the idea. The French are good at this stuff, just as they're also good at doing mad things like the Renault Avantime and that DS5 which pretends it's not a Citroën and seems to have too many sunroofs. The French may have had a few wobbles in recent years, not least from Peugeot who appeared to lose the sporty yet comfortable plot for a while, but the spongy, bungy Citroën C4 Cactus and hilariously lively Peugeot 308 GTi show all is not lost.

GERMANY

Current annual production:
6 million

Epicentre: Stuttgart

Most famous cars:
Mercedes 300SL, VW Golf, VW Beetle, BMW M3, BMW 507, Mercedes S-class, und many more.

Best current model:
Take your pick

Germany has no trouble laying claim to being a great car-making nation on account of, oh you know, basically inventing the car. Germany's real skill, however, seems to be taking basic ideas from elsewhere, making them work properly, and then selling them to a world that is in love with the reassuring thunk of sensible Germanic engineering. The Beetle didn't invent carefully engineered rear-engined motoring for the masses. The Golf GTI didn't invent the hot hatchback. BMW didn't even invent the idea of small, sporty saloon cars for people with 'executive' in their job title. But in each case the Germans finished the job and made it a success. It's a trick they're still pulling off today, which is why, though someone else first had the idea of making a sensible, practical, medium-sized hatchback, whenever you need to recommend one to a friend you end up telling them to buy a Golf.

SWEDEN

Current annual production:
200,000

Epicentre: Gothenburg

Most famous cars:
SAAB 99 Turbo, Volvo 850R,
Koenigsegg CCX

Best current model:
Koenigsegg Regera

Sweden doesn't make very many cars and frankly never has. But that's not the point. It doesn't have very many people either and yet it managed to turn out Björn Borg and ABBA. Quality, not quantity. And just look at the quality of cars Sweden has turned out over the years. Not the prettiest, not the fastest, not the sportiest, but certainly the nicest. If you're a stickler for a logical dashboard, a tremendously comfortable seat and projecting a calm, quiet, thoughtful image, you want your car to be from Sweden.

Not that the Swedes are boring, you understand. Every so often they come up with something fast like the SAAB 99 Turbo or the Koenigsegg CCX, cars that are only made more fun for coming from the land of extremely crisp instrument markings and griddle-spec heated seats. Sadly, SAAB is no longer with us, but Sweden still does what it's always done. Quality, not quantity.

CHINA

Current annual production: 28 million

Epicentre: Wuhan

Most famous cars: Citroën Fukang, Roewe 750, all those ones that look suspiciously like European cars but aren't

Best current model: Lynk & Co 01

In car-making terms, China is one of the world's new boys. Just 30 years ago they made about 5,000 cars a year. Now their annual car output is greater than that of the USA and Japan put together. No one builds more cars than the Chinese, which is quite an achievement. Of course, it's very easy to smirk at their car industry and to claim that it just makes rubbish copies of Western cars called funny things like the Wang Bang Maximum Sex Monkey 8000, all of which look like a Daewoo Matiz that's crashed into a plastic slide. But that's not the case any more. The Chinese are learning fast and their design work is getting more original just as their car names are getting more comprehensible. Let's also not forget that the Chinese now own MG, Volvo, Lotus and the people who build the famous London black cabs. They're also forging ahead with new tech, including electric cars, at a pace that would embarrass the old guard. Underestimate the Chinese at your peril.

INDIA

Current annual production: 4.5 million

Epicentre: Chennai

Most famous cars: Hindustan Ambassador, Premier Padmini

Best current model: Tata Nano

India has had a car industry for a long time, but for years it was represented by just a handful of companies making local versions of outdated Morrises and Fiats. Over time, they bought in some new designs but these too were other people's leftovers, mostly the random cast-offs of the British car industry such as the Rover SD1, Austin Montego and Reliant Kitten. None did remotely as well as the famous Hindustan Ambassador, a 1950s Morris Oxford that seemed to make up 90 per cent of Indian urban traffic. But all that has changed, and the Indian car industry is coming up with its own stuff now, led by Tata, who not only create their own designs, including the

ingenious low-cost Nano, but also own Britain's Jaguar and Land Rover. India has also quietly become an R&D centre for the global car industry and, because it's never forgotten good old-fashioned craftsmanship, is also where at least one well-known Euro car maker has had flashy motor show concepts made. Meanwhile, the Ambassador finally went out of production in 2014 and the name has now been bought by Peugeot. Austin didn't want it back on account of being dead.

The world makes about 90 million cars every year. That's almost 250,000 cars every single day.

SOUTH KOREA

Current annual production:
4.2 million

Epicentre: Ulsan

Most famous cars:
Hyundai Pony, Kia Pride,
Hyundai Coupe, Kia Cee'd

Best current model:
Kia Stinger

One of the world's newcomers in car-making terms, before 1975 South Korea had little home-grown car industry to speak of. Then industrial conglomerate Hyundai decided to change that and hired a former British Leyland bigwig to make it so. The end result was basically a nicer-looking Morris Marina, engineered by Mitsubishi staff earning money on the side by flying to South Korea at weekends. It was called the Pony and it wasn't very good. Nor was their next car, the Stellar, which was a re-hashed Ford Cortina. But Hyundai, and South Korea, learned fast. With a combination of low prices and long warranties, they got a foot in the door and then improved their styling and engineering beyond belief in order to kick that door down. Now Hyundai-Kia is the third-biggest vehicle maker in the world. Pretty impressive for a company that had yet to design its own car in the year Ford celebrated its 70th birthday. Of course, although Hyundai and Kia are the core of today's South Korean car industry, you can't forget SsangYong. Look, I know you've tried. God knows, we all have. But you can't forget SsangYong. Sorry.

JAPAN

Current annual production:
9 million

Epicentre: Nagoya

Most famous cars:
Toyota 2000GT, Honda NSX,
Nissan 240Z, Lexus LFA,
Toyota Corolla, and so on

Best current model:
Honda NSX

Germany may lay claim to inventing the car and America may have got it into affordable mass production, but Japan is the place that made it work properly. Being so obsessed with doors that fitted and engines that ran without needing constant attention may have gained the Japanese a reputation for being a bit boring back when owners of American and European cars couldn't take such things for granted, but the Japanese have always been able to pull a little something special out of their beautifully made back pockets just to show that they're not dullards. Hence, full-house classics like the Nissan 240Z or the Toyota 2000GT. And the accusation that the Japanese are copycats isn't entirely fair either because there's nothing on earth that drives like the glorious Lexus LFA, nor indeed anything that looks like it. Of course, there's nothing else that looks like the current Toyota Prius either, and for that we should be thankful. But even Japan's most manky-looking cars are precisely engineered and impeccably made, both of which explain why half the world relies on Toyota Hiluxes and the other half is happily on to its third Corolla.

POSTCARD

FROM THE TENT

Having an amazing time here in California. Pitched the tent in a place called Apple Valley, which doesn't seem to have any apples in it. Mostly just desert.

Got here the day before cameras rolled so we all went out to see the set. Presenters couldn't believe all the brilliant cars we'd got lined up – spent a couple of hours just wandering about looking at them and taking pictures. We really liked the Vector. Next day we had to film the big opening sequence. Couldn't believe a mad idea Jeremy had in the office was all coming true. Cars, planes, fire-breathing metal dragons and fighter planes. Hothouse Flowers played other songs in the breaks to amuse the audience. Top band. The following day we filmed the bit inside the tent. Killed a few celebrities but it all went well. When it was done and the audience

had gone home, the presenters went out into the crowd-holding tent with some beers and sat on hay bales watching the sun go down and taking it in turns to pretend to be dead. Carol Vorderman came with us but she'd already been dead today so she pretended to be alive. Happy times.

See you soon,

THE GRAND TOUR

GRAND TOUR TOP OF THE COPS

PORSCHE 911 TARGA

COUNTRY	THE NETHERLANDS
TOP SPEED	152 MPH
0-62 MPH	6.1 SECONDS

Some time ago the Dutch police went to their governmental superiors and told them, with a completely straight face, that they needed air-cooled, rear-engined cars because anything front-engined and water-cooled might overheat if required to reverse at high speed in an emergency. Oh, and these cars also needed a removable roof in case an officer needed to stand on the seat to direct traffic. Funnily enough, the only model that fitted this unusually specific brief was the Porsche 911 Targa. And, amazingly, the government said yes. What's the Dutch for 'ballsy'?

WORLD'S BEST POLICE CARS

BUGATTI VEYRON

COUNTRY	DUBAI
TOP SPEED	253 MPH
0-62 MPH	2.5 SECONDS

Nothing is going to drive you as quickly down the thin blue line as a 1,000-horsepower Bugatti, and hats (or helmets) off to the Dubai police force for being alone in recognising this. Yes, it's not very practical for multiple arrests and is pretty much just a PR exercise, but in that respect it's a damn sight more effective than a poster that says, 'Burgled? Call 9 double 9!'

HAVE YOU CONSIDERED THE...
HOT-AIR BALLOON?

There are lots of ways to cover big distances around the world, from cars to boats to aeroplanes. But most people overlook another excellent way to travel – the hot-air balloon. Just look at some of the advantages of making your next long-distance trip by hot-air balloon:

'We appear to be drifting out to sea.'

'Stop being such a massive... Oh yeah, you're right.'

- Drift peacefully over land or sea
- Very quiet (apart from that noisy burner thing)
- Literally impossible to control
- Won't go in the direction you want
- Vastly increased risk of drifting into power lines

When planning your next trip, don't forget to travel by hot-air balloon. The only way to travel for anyone who wants to call the people they were supposed to be having a meeting with in order to explain that they're late because they've drifted out to sea in a massive exclamation mark again.

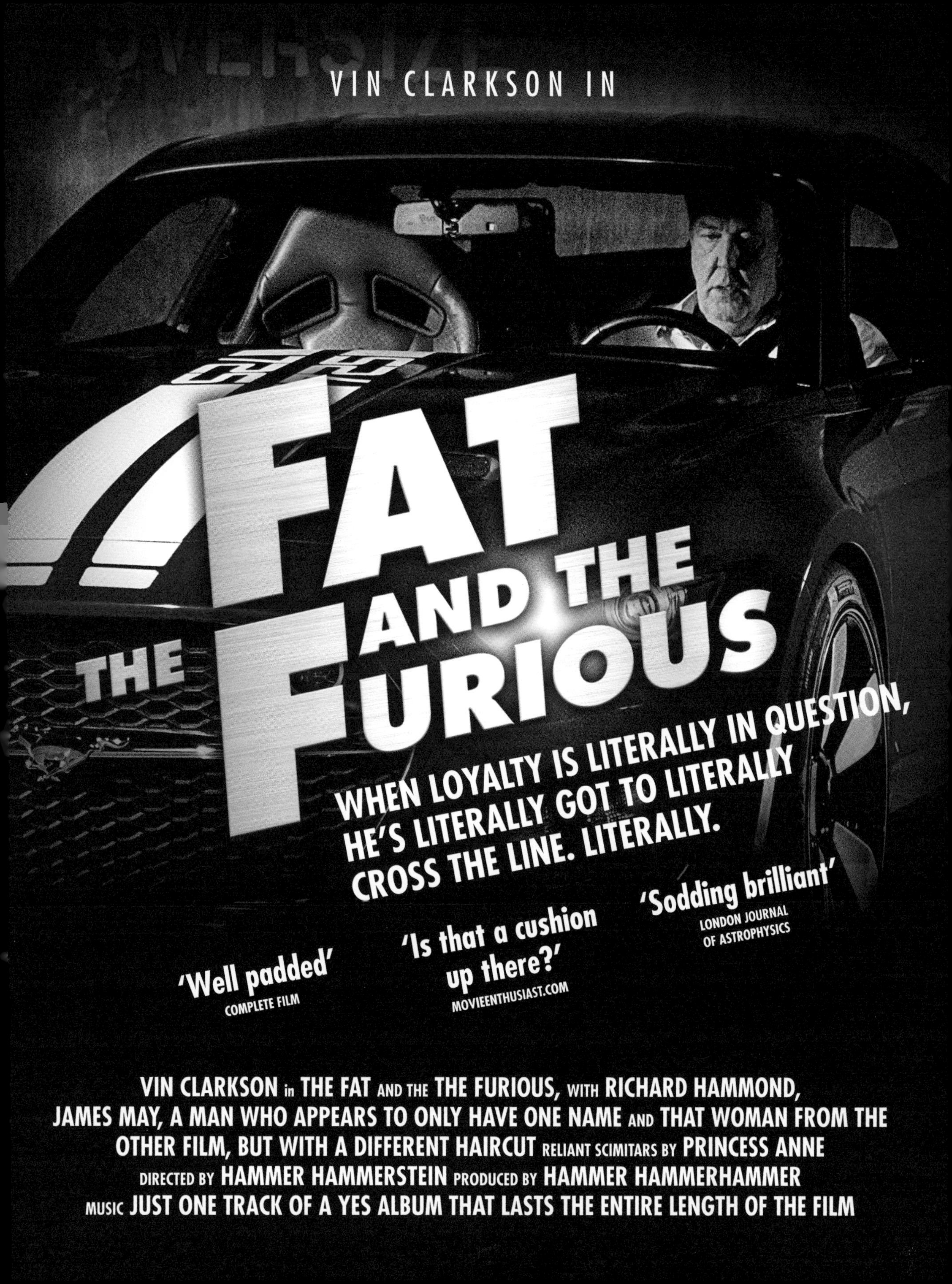
VIN CLARKSON IN
THE FAT AND THE FURIOUS
WHEN LOYALTY IS LITERALLY IN QUESTION, HE'S LITERALLY GOT TO LITERALLY CROSS THE LINE. LITERALLY.
'Well padded' COMPLETE FILM
'Is that a cushion up there?' MOVIEENTHUSIAST.COM
'Sodding brilliant' LONDON JOURNAL OF ASTROPHYSICS
VIN CLARKSON in THE FAT AND THE THE FURIOUS, WITH RICHARD HAMMOND, JAMES MAY, A MAN WHO APPEARS TO ONLY HAVE ONE NAME AND THAT WOMAN FROM THE OTHER FILM, BUT WITH A DIFFERENT HAIRCUT RELIANT SCIMITARS BY PRINCESS ANNE
DIRECTED BY HAMMER HAMMERSTEIN PRODUCED BY HAMMER HAMMERHAMMER
MUSIC JUST ONE TRACK OF A YES ALBUM THAT LASTS THE ENTIRE LENGTH OF THE FILM

PIT STOP 03

JORDAN

FOCUS ON JORDAN

RUSSIA
HUGE AND OFTEN COLD

EUROPE
MEDIUM SIZED, A MIX OF TEMPERATURES

PETROL

THE
MIDDLE
EAST
QUITE LARGE AND
QUITE WARM

AFRICA
MASSIVE AND OOOH IT
CAN GET TOASTY

a.k.a.

AL-URDUNN OR THE HASHEMITE KINGDOM OF JORDAN

Jordan is home to a unique military facility dedicated to making television features that viewers don't like.

Population:

10 MILLION

Jordan the country should not be confused with Jordan the pneumatic chest nuisance.

JORDAN IS HOME TO THE ANCIENT CITY OF PETRA, BETTER KNOWN AS 'THAT PLACE FROM THAT INDIANA JONES FILM'.

Currency:

JORDANIAN DINAR

The 2015 Matt Damon film *The Martian* was not filmed on Mars but in Jordan. Unlike the 2000 documentary film *Michael Jordan to the Max*, which, ironically, was shot on Mars.

Capital:

AMMAN

The traditional dish of Jordan is mansaf, which is lamb cooked in fermented yoghurt and seasoned with paprika and cumin, served with flatbread and rice. Or, if you're Richard Hammond, you could just have cheese on toast.

Jordan the country should not be confused with Jordan the Formula One team run by an unusually clothed speaking enthusiast.

Famous people:
KING HUSSEIN OF JORDAN, KING ABDULLAH II OF JORDAN, QUEEN RANIA OF JORDAN

BEHIND THE SCENES

In one of their most ambitious endeavours to date, Jeremy, Richard and James went to Jordan to try their hand at being super army soldiers. How many times did they die? Who knows? Did anyone care? Erm...

Double camera coverage as a middle-aged man in ill-fitting camo gear slowly peels a quail's egg in the middle of a military training base. All perfectly normal.

Actual Jeremy dangles from an actual helicopter, moments before losing his actual trousers.

James May strafes the airliner. A phrase we all knew we'd hear one day.

Weapons used in this film include SIG Sauer P226, G&P MK18 Mod 0, M4 carbine and FN Minimi. Total number of rounds used during filming: 6,900.

Above, Jeremy in unusually jaunty mood for someone who has just been hosed down with relentless gunfire.

Jeremy gets molested by unseen terrorists. Amazon were (unsurprisingly) quite perplexed by this scene on first viewing.

Below, Hammond wallops Clarkson in the head with a shovel. Just like in all of his sweet, sweet dreams.

Above, James hangs out with a pretend Queen Elizabeth II only by suppressing his pretend inner republican.

FAMOUS JORDANS

The country of Jordan isn't the only famous Jordan. There are other ones too, such as Jordan. Here is a list.

JORDAN KNIGHT

Singer, dancer, old kid
on the block

JORDAN

Model, author,
specifically
bulbous person

JORDAN BELFORT

Stockbroker, author,
wolf (of Wall St.)

JORDIN SPARKS

Singer, songwriter, fairly
atrocious speller

JORDAN, MICHAEL

Basketballist and air-
based training-shoe
enthusiast

EDDIE JORDAN

Pundit, team owner,
constant speaking noise

JORDAN CLARKSON

Basketball player.
No, really, look it up

JORDAN

First Bishop of Poland.
No, really, look it up

JORDANS

Apostrophe-phobic maker
of breakfast cereal

YOU DO REALISE THE MONARCHY IS ESSENTIALLY AN OUTMODED CONCEPT?
YOU DO REALISE I'M GOING TO HAVE YOU BEHEADED?

FILMS WITH JEREMY CLARKSON

Travelling is boring. Fortunately, you can make it more unboring by watching a good film. But what is a good film? Well, don't worry, I've come up with this handy film assessment system that will help to make up your mind. Simply answer the questions opposite and you'll know for certain if the film you're watching is any good.

HAS THERE BEEN A MINIMUM OF TWO CAR CHASES?

And did one of the car chases start with someone jumping in front of a random car and then commandeering it with the words, 'I'm going to need your vehicle. The president is in danger'?

HAVE ANY OF THE CHARACTERS USED ONE OR MORE OF THE FOLLOWING PHRASES?

'Secure the perimeter', 'The cordon has been compromised', 'Patch it to my PDA', 'Not on my watch', 'FREEZE! FBI!'

HAS A MAN FALLEN OUT OF A PLANE BUT AS HE'S FALLING HE'S STILL FIRING BACK AT THE PLANE?

DID THE LEAD CHARACTER SMASH A BADDY IN THE FACE WITH A SECURITY BARRIER...

...and then say 'access denied' (or similar)?

DOES SOMEONE FIRE TWO AUTOMATIC WEAPONS INTO A ROOM AT ONCE WITH THEIR ARMS CROSSED?

DO SOME BIRDS TAKE OFF IN SLOW MOTION FOR NO READILY APPARENT REASON?

If you can answer yes to at least three of these questions, it's probably a good film.

POSTCARD

FROM THE TENT

Hello from North Yorkshire. Had a great drive here across the moors in a load of hot hatchbacks led by Jeremy, who is an evangelist for the A170 road. With good reason, because it's brilliant. He also claimed to know the best fish and chip shop in Whitby so we went there only to find some of our crew had got in first and eaten all of the large cod. Jeremy compensated for this by ordering two small cods and wolfing them down, but then ruined the impressive effect by washing it all down with a small fizzy lager. Richard and James got it right by having proper brown Northern beer. Had fish and chips again for lunch next day. First studio recording went

well. Had fish and chips for dinner. Still wasn't bored of it. Next day, another studio recording. Doing two here because we like it so much. Also, it's less expensive than going abroad again. Had fish and chips for lunch. Might be addicted to fish and chips. Another great audience for second show. Feels like being home. More fish and chips for dinner. Might have to take some back to the office. See you soon,

THE GRAND TOUR

WORLD'S BEST POLICE CARS

VOLVO V70

COUNTRY	SWEDEN
TOP SPEED	121 MPH
0-62 MPH	10.6 SECONDS

If television drama has taught us anything it's that Swedish policing mostly involves driving about on very long, straight roads under very wide, bleak skies while wearing a jumper and then stopping for a bit to stare at a lake while sighing. And what better machine in which to do that than the ultra-pleasant Volvo V70? So comfortable, so spacious, so perfect for leaning on while gazing wistfully at a large, grey body of water. Pfffffffffff.

ALFA ROMEO GIULIA QUADRIFOGLIO

COUNTRY	ITALY
TOP SPEED	191 MPH
0-62 MPH	3.9 SECONDS

The main job of the Italian police is to look cool, but all the sunglasses and chewing gum in the world couldn't help them when they had to jump into a Fiat Croma or Alfa Giulietta diesel. Thankfully, the Giulia Quadrifoglia is here to save them with its farty, half-Ferrari V6 engine and powersliding rear-wheel-drive chassis. Being an Italian cop has never looked so appealing. Expect to see Milanese law enforcement by Commandore Jeremi Clarksonio any day now.

TRAVEL TIPS

Getting an Upgrade

Getting an airline upgrade is the dream of any traveller, whether it's getting bumped upwards from economy to business, from business to first, or from first to being allowed to fly the plane. But airlines don't hand out such things willy-nilly. In fact, they generally don't hand them out at all unless it is in exchange for something called 'money'. But don't despair. There are certain insiders' tips and tricks that can help you to achieve that dream upgrade for free. Just follow as many as possible of the examples opposite and in no time you'll be sitting slightly nearer the impact!

A plane of dummies. And also some plastic life-sized models of people.

Use the power of suggestion by legally changing your name to 'Mr Upgrade' or, for more powerful effect, 'Lord Upgrade-Now'.

Gain access to any part of the plane you want by becoming a member of the cabin crew.

Walk straight into first class while loudly shouting, 'I AM THE KATE MOSS.'

Gain access to the first-class cabin by disguising yourself as a real metal knife or quilted eye mask.

Bring your own fully reclining bed seat, complimentary gin and tonics and fillet steak, and enjoy them in economy.

Become a pilot. No one sits nearer the front than pilots.

Claim to have a 'medical condition' that makes it vital that you can have a lie-down and a free glass of Scotch if you want to.

ITALY

FOCUS ON ITALY

RUSSIA
MOSTLY NOT PART OF EUROPE.PROBABLY DOESN'T WANT TO BE

ITALY
THE PART OF EUROPE THAT LOOKS LIKE A BOOT

EUROPE
ALL OF THIS BIT

PETROL

AFRICA
JUST MINDING ITS OWN BUSINESS DOWN HERE

a.k.a.

ITALIA

The Italians are responsible for Fiat, Ferrari, Lancia, Alfa Romeo, De Tomaso, Lamborghini, Maserati and Pagani. It wouldn't seem so unfair if they weren't also really good at food, art and fashion. Selfish. That's what it is, it's selfish.

Population:

60 MILLION

At its height, the Roman Empire stretched from Portugal to Syria and from North Africa to the top of England. But the Scottish told them to sod off.

An Italian politician automatically receives a long-service medal if they have not been killed or bought off after their first day in office.

Capital:

ROME

The Italian word for 'lunch' is the same as the Italian word for 'very civilised two-hour break in the middle of the day'.

Currency:

EURO

According to Richard Hammond, the Italian word for 'pizza' is, amazingly, 'pizza'.

Fans of the Ferrari Formula One team are known as the 'tifosi'. This word literally means 'covered in branded clothing'.

Famous people:

SILVIO BERLUSCONI,

Valentino Rossi, Enzo Ferrari, Ferruccio Lamborghini, Carla Bruni, Leonardo da Vinci, a lot of artists and footballers.

BEHIND THE SCENES

When Jeremy and James decided to go on a gentlemanly grand tour of Italy in two cars that are refined and civilised, they didn't bank on the company of Richard Hammond, who isn't, and a Dodge Charger Hellcat, which isn't either.

The international symbol for 'loser'. Unless you accidentally use your left hand, then it's the international symbol for 'juice box'.

The Aston Martin DB11, resplendent in brown or orange, depending on how colour blind and belligerent you are.

The Rolls-Royce Dawn doesn't come with a DSLR camera in the back seat. We put that there for filming.

James May preparing to set off, a process that can take up to four days.

Above, Richard Hammond poses with his work. He went to art college, you know. Right, James May poses with his cunning disguise. He didn't go to disguise college, you know.

Jeremy and James are pulled from the waters of Venice and into the welcome arms of our crew (right). James later admitted that he really thought he was going to drown.

Left, James does some painting. Of a thing that's to his right. Logical easel placement not a strong point.

Right, Clarkson very subtly expresses his feelings about Hammond arriving.

THE ITALIAN CAR
CLICHÉ-O-METER

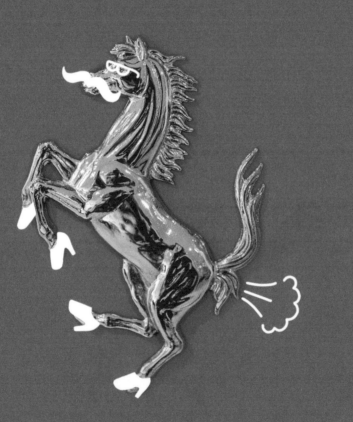

Whenever anyone tests an Italian car it is an unofficial requirement for them to trot out the same clichés everyone has been using for 50 years. Here is your guide to the strength of cliché you may encounter when reading any road test of an Italian car.

3 MINUTES WITH ...

RICHARD HAMMOND

A rapid-fire Q&A with the local radio DJ turned *Grand Tour* presenter

WILL CHILDREN READ THIS BOOK?

HELLO, RICHARD.

Hello!

So, first question: Jeremy Clarkson – can you sum him up in three words?
Will children read this book?

They might.
Oh. Oh dear. That's going to be tricky then. Can we come back to this one?

Of course. What about James May? Can you sum him up in three words?
Are children still reading?

They might be.
Riiiiight. Might have to come back to this one too. Sorry.

That's okay. Here's an easier one. Sum up *The Grand Tour* in three words.
Erm, okay, right. Tele ... vision ... show.

That's two words.
Oh, okay. Tele ... vision ... show ... about ... cars.

That's four words.
No, I'm using 'television show' as one word.

But 'television show' isn't one word.
It is to some people.

Which people?
Me. Ah-ha, didn't think of that did you?

No. But, with respect, that's not really a cogent argument. Just because one person thinks or does

something doesn't make it correct.
Alright, James May. I didn't realise this interview was called 'three minutes in which someone comes into Richard's office and is really pedantic about stuff'.

Speaking of which, time is short and we should move on. I have to ask, when I was interviewing Jeremy there was a noise outside and he claimed it was you falling down the stairs. Is that correct?
Oh for God's sake, you have one little accident or two and they want to make out like you're some kind of bungling Inspector Clouseau character who can't do a single thing without turning it into a massive farce. It's simply not true.

In fairness, and I wasn't going to mention this, you seem to have a stapler stuck to your sleeve.

Yes, I know. I put it there. Deliberately.

So you didn't fall down the stairs earlier?

Well I might have, a little bit. But that's not the point. Everyone falls down the stairs once or twice a day.

Do they?

Yes. Yes they do. I know I do. It doesn't make me accident prone. Likewise, the stapler. Did you know that stapling mishaps kill more people in Britain every year than other common accidents such as trying to drink from a tap and accidentally turning the tap on too much and then loads of water comes out of your nose and then you almost drown to death.

I've never heard of that happening to anyone.

It happens all the time. It's happened to me twice this week alone. Taps are lethal.

And stairs.

I don't want to dwell on the stairs. And I mean that quite literally. But yes, they're lethal. Look, my point is that I'm not some kind of flailing buffoon, some sort of Norman Wisdom character. I mean, look, this window here has been open the whole time I've been talking to you and have I fallen out of it?

No, I suppose not.

Exactly. You listen to the other two and they're always saying, 'Oh, don't let Hammond near open windows. Let's move Hammond's office off the first floor. Let's put child

locks on all the taps and stop storing anvils on that shelf' and it's nonsense.

Yes, I see. So, to get back to the original question. Can you describe Jeremy Clarkson in three words?

I think I'm going to go with 'That bloody Jeremy Clarkson'.

That's four words.

No, I'm using Jeremy Clarkson as one word.

But it … actually, I think we're out of time.

Oh, okay. Well, nice to talk to you. Let me show you out … arrrgh!

Richard falls out of the window.

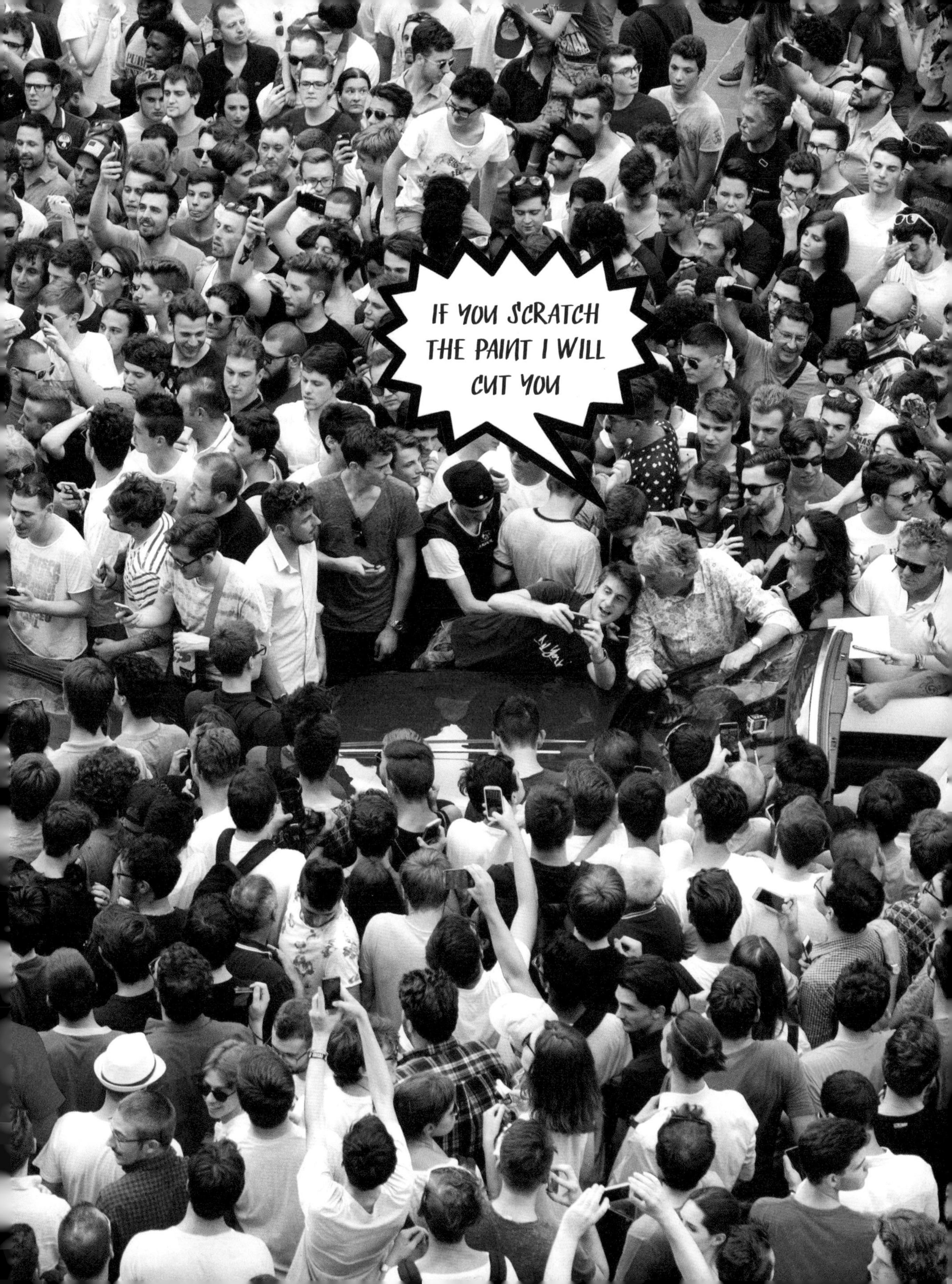
IF YOU SCRATCH THE PAINT I WILL CUT YOU

CLARKSOTOURS

FOR THE LOW-ATTENTION-SPAN TRAVELLER

'LITERALLY, COME ON HOLIDAY WITH ME'

'I've been travelling the world for ages and most of it is extremely dull. But don't worry, we'll skirt past all that, have a quick look at some interesting rocks and be in the bar before sun down.' Jeremy

Clarksotours is Britain's number one holiday tour company.* But don't just take our word for it; ask our founder, Jeremy Clarkson.

THE LOUVRE

'It's just pictures, they're all the same.'

THE PYRAMIDS

'I've no idea what these are, but they're not interesting. Come on, come on, keep moving.'

DOLPHINS

'Look, if they were that clever they would have cars by now.'

* According to a poll conducted in Jeremy Clarkson's mind.

WORLD'S BEST POLICE CARS

HOLDEN COMMODORE SS

COUNTRY	AUSTRALIA
TOP SPEED	149 MPH
0-62 MPH	4.9 SECONDS

A no-nonsense place like Australia needs a no-nonsense police car, and that's just what they've got with the V8-powered, rear-wheel-drive Commodore. Unfortunately, Commodore production ended in October 2017, with no direct replacement in the field of cars that are as simple as a steak and just as meaty. That means cop Commodores will start to disappear, to be replaced by weedier cars with lesser engines. As a result, all crime in Australia will probably stop simply because everyone is just too sad.

BRABUS CLS V12

COUNTRY	GERMANY
TOP SPEED	227 MPH
0-62 MPH	3.2 SECONDS

Germany is one of the few places in the world where you can legally drive a car as fast as possible. Perhaps that's why German police ordered up this V12 sledgehammer, confected by the thinking person's Merc tuner, Brabus. Mind you, police in Berlin use Toyota Priuses so if you're thinking of committing a crime in Germany and you want to get away, head to Berlin and learn to run reasonably quickly.

WHY NOT DRIVE?

Planes and boats are all well and good but for some reason the people who run them never let you have a go at the controls. That's why cars are better, as emeritus professor of travel Dr J.C.R. Clarkson explains...

If you're travelling around the world it's generally accepted that the best way is to fly. But hold on a second. Flying means having to get to an airport and airports are never near your house. Flying means having to remove your jacket and your belt and take all the things out of your pockets and generally dismantle your life to a molecular level. Flying means hanging around a sort of narrow shopping centre for two hours waiting to get onto a thin tube full of other people's germs. Flying means delays and turbulence and boredom and the lingering fear in the back of your mind that this might be the time you should have said a proper goodbye to your loved ones and got your affairs in order and admitted to those around you that you've never seen *The Usual Suspects*. In short, flying is a pain in the bottom. But there is an answer: next time you're going away, just drive. The advantages of driving are many. You can leave when you want. You don't have to sit next to a stranger. You can listen to all sorts of loud music without headphones and look at things out of the window that aren't just clouds. Driving is a sensible alternative to flying, despite what James says. So let's see how the driving option stacks up on a trip from London to LA.

LONDON TO LOS ANGELES

FLYING

Take taxi to Heathrow airport. Check in. Pass through security. Wait for ages in airport. Trudge around wasting money on magazines and complicated coffees. Get on plane. Discover you are sitting next to what appears to be a walrus in a Metallica T-shirt. Sit for ages on tarmac. Take off. Fly for 10 or 11 long, boring hours next to the snoring walrus. Land at Los Angeles airport. Sit on plane as it taxis for what feels like about an hour. Get off plane. Queue for what feels like 100 hours at immigration. Wait for another 120 hours in baggage reclaim. Wait another 290 hours in the queue to hand in that inexplicable customs slip. Get out of airport. Wait for 400 hours for bus to car-hire depot. Get to car-hire depot. Spend the rest of your natural life filling in forms for car hire. Die.

DRIVING

Get up when you want. Set off when you want. Head to Channel Tunnel. Get on car train, pop out in France. Set sat-nav for Los Angeles. Drive across Europe and Russia (warning: Russia is quite big, so remember to bring some snacks). Get ferry across Bering Strait to Alaska (warning: there is no ferry service at the moment, so remember to bring your own). Drive to Los Angeles.

Added bonus: People always say, 'Oooh, you can't get around LA without a car.' Well, you've just turned up with your own. Take that, car-hire companies.

POSTCARD

FROM THE TENT

Arrived yesterday in Rotterdam. Still unsettled by the sight of the presenters in a corner of the hotel bar gleefully showing off a suitcase full of 'adult' items bought from an 'adult' shop of the kind that people sometimes associate with the Netherlands.

The tent is pitched in a container yard on the docks. Place is massive and it's full of cranes that work automatically and autonomous container lorries that drive around with no one in them. Like a spooky but very organised version of the future. Started rehearsing in the studio and then discovered that all the huge automated cranes outside beep when they move. And they move a lot. One of our producers went to ask if they could be stopped while we were filming

the show because it was going to ruin our sound recording. The container yard people said that might take a while because all of these Dutch cranes are controlled from a nerve centre. Which is in Hong Kong. The future is mad. Show went well. Team went back to hotel bar for several adult beverages. But no more 'adult' toys. Don't know what happened to them. Hmm. See you soon,

THE GRAND TOUR

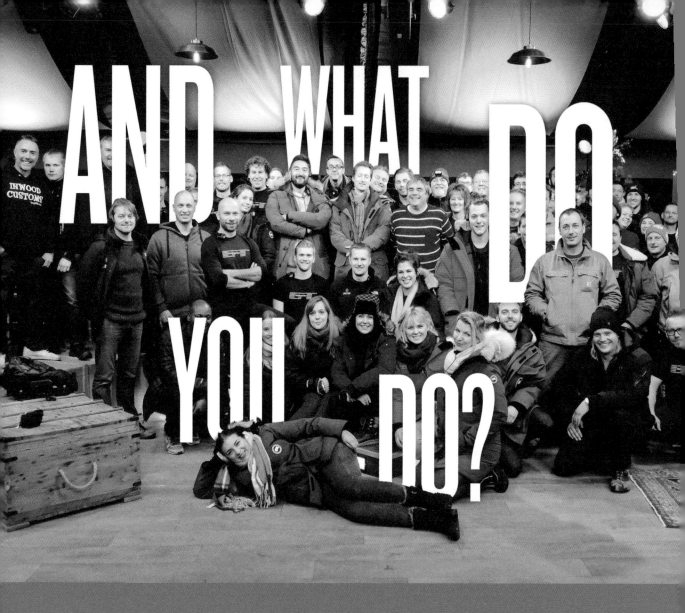

AND WHAT DO YOU DO?

The Grand Tour couldn't function without its production team, the names of whom you'll see in the closing credits to the show. But there are also several uncredited people who work tirelessly behind the scenes on some of the less well-known jobs. These are those people.

ERIEL MUNN
JAMES'S CAT PERSON

CRESSIDA TEASBY
RICHARD'S
DIALOGUE COACH

t's a little-known fact that TV's James May insists on having access to cats wherever he goes. This requirement has become ever-more important recently, to the extent that May has it written into his contract that at any given time there will be at least seven cats for him to scritch in that weird soft fluffy bit at the side of their heads. This can be problematic since TV's Jeremy Clarkson is allergic to cats, but the issue is solved by Eriel Munn, who follows James around with a specially designed 'cat capsule' full of cats, into which he can disappear at a moment's notice. Hence, once the director calls cut on a take, May will often roar, 'Get me pussy,' and Munn will appear with the furiously mewing orb of animals. This is not to be mistaken for anything else. He's not Donald Trump.

t was said that in periods of inactivity, Keith Moon of The Who would forget how to play the drums and had to 're-learn' for every new tour or album recording. Well, the same is true of TV's Richard Hammond, but it's not drumming that he forgets; it's the letter 'W'. That's where Cressida Teasby comes in. As a new recording starts, Richard will often turn to camera and say, 'Elcome to this eek's show, and just look ott ee've got for you to otch.' In times past, the crew would panic, recording would be cancelled and all the expensive cameras thrown into a canal. But not any more, because whenever Richard suffers from what doctors call 'W forgetting syndrome', Teasby quickly sneaks onto the set and whispers the correct sentence into his ear. The production team know all will be fine, and she can stand down until the next time they're on location and hear Richard call Jeremy an 'anchor'.

KENDAL WHUMS

HORSE REPELLER

Wherever *The Grand Tour* goes in the world it is sure to attract a crowd of fans and possibly the attention of the police. But there's something else the show attracts, and it's something much more dangerous and unwanted. We're talking of course about horses. Wherever Jeremy, Richard and James are in the world, an unwanted flock of horses is sure to be close behind. Unfortunately, this causes great problems when filming, and indeed off-camera. They whinny during crucial pieces to camera. Their clip-clopping feet compromise sound quality. And they often insist on trying to follow the team into restaurants, even if there is a sign on the door clearly saying 'NO HORSES'. That's where Kendal Whums comes in, permanently on duty to shoo away the horses, which he's able to do in over 13 languages. Whums is also engaged in an ongoing project to find out why *The Grand Tour* is so plagued by the horse menace. His latest theory is that they like the smell of the special marker pens used to label memory cards.

LESTON VESTIBULE

ORNAMENTS

Keen-eyed viewers will have noticed a large number of old signs, maps, books, globes and other ornaments that pepper the interior of *The Grand Tour* tent, making it look nice and homely. What the audience at home don't know is that after a recording each and every single piece of set dressing has to be smashed, crushed and then burned for various reasons, mostly relating to hygiene. That poses a big problem for the show's Head of Ornaments, Leston Vestibule, who then has to go out and find a whole pile of identical pieces with which to dress the set at the next recording. 'It's a bloody nightmare,' he admits, 'but I suppose you could say I'm instrumental in the making of the show. No, wait, sorry, I meant to say "ornamental in the making of the show". Damn. I've been planning that one for ages. Sorry.'

JOHAN KREEE

TENT-DOOR SPECIALIST

I f you've watched the beginning of any episode of *The Grand Tour* you'll have noticed that the presenters enter the tent through a large entrance way. But look closer and you'll notice something amazing about that entrance way: the door that covers it doesn't open sideways like a normal door; it retracts upwards like the door from a space ship or something. How does this magic work? Well, it's an extremely complicated system based around a massive flap of canvas and some string. But this alone would not permit the presentational team access to their place of work just as everyone starts clapping. Such an unusual and sophisticated mechanism needs a specialist to operate it, and that's where Johan Kreee comes in. He's the only member of the crew with the skill and the training to pull on the piece of string at exactly the right time to make the magical door work. 'It's a very technical job,' he quips. 'And if anyone else tried to do it, they would be killed instantly.'

ECHRON POBE

JEREMY'S TROUSER
WRANGLER

J ournalist, author, broadcaster. Jeremy Clarkson has many strings to his bow. Yet few realise that despite his many talents, Clarkson is harbouring a dark secret – he doesn't know how trousers work. For many years he kept this hidden, even from his co-hosts, and if required to change trousers backstage would sneak off to a hidden room and ask a member of the production team to help him with 'these long flappy bits' or to insert himself into 'the, you know, leg pipe things'. These days Jeremy's affliction is better known and understood among the crew, and with that understanding comes a dedicated person who can help him put on and take off trousers. The trouser wrangler will even attempt to coach Jeremy into a better understanding of trousers with gentle encouragement, such as 'There's no need to put your head in there' and 'Strictly speaking there's no such thing as "the arse hammock",' though it's probably too late for all that.

TAKING A CAMERA

T
—
W

If you're travelling the world you'll probably want to capture your experiences on video but picking the right camera and format can be a real head-scratcher.

Fortunately, *The Grand Tour* is here to help. For filming outdoors we would use Arri Amiras and Panasonic GH4s shooting in super high definition 4K HDR for a pin-sharp image. The HDR part is very important here since it means every single frame of footage is actually three frames taken at the same time but with different levels of exposure to give even higher definition. It's a system that'll really make your footage 'pop'. You'll also want to run your cameras at a movie-standard frame rate of 23.98 frames per second rather than the traditional 25p to give everything a really filmic quality.

For indoor filming we would try a suite of Sony HDC-4300s running the same tech specs, feeding into custom-made servers that can fit into flight cases for ease of transport wherever you are in the world.

If you're out in the field, obviously you'll be merrily shooting away so it's worth travelling with a team of three data wranglers who can ingest the footage from your memory cards into high-powered laptops and then back it up to a series of extra-tough portable hard drives, remembering that each terabyte of data takes about 20 hours to transfer. That's important to remember because if you're away for two weeks in, say, Namibia, you'll probably generate about 40 terabytes of raw data or enough to fill around 80 normal laptops. It's also worth remembering that when you get home and you want to edit your footage, you should probably book a high-end edit facility in London's Soho district and remember that, when moving the footage into their computers, just one series of travels could result in over 6,000 hours of ingest time!

On the plus side, your holiday films will look amazing! Even if they have Jeremy Clarkson in them!

Below, two examples of the kind of compact and inexpensive camera you should take on holiday.

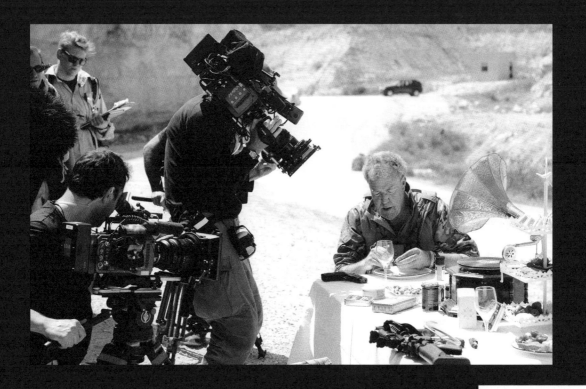

PIT STOP 05

WALES

FOCUS ON WALES

SCANDINAVIA
LOVELY, BUT BRRRR

WALES
HOME OF SPIT

EUROPE
CONTAINS FRANCE, SPAIN, GERMANY...
ACTUALLY, FORGET IT, THIS WILL TAKE
FAR TOO LONG

a.k.a.

CYMRU (IF YOU'RE WELSH)

The longest word in Welsh is 'llllanalllllllllalllllllly-lllllllllllllllalllllylllllllllylnnall-lllyngnth', which means 'small stain on a marble work surface'.

Population:

3 MILLION

THE NATURAL CLIMATE OF WALES IS OF A TYPE KNOWN TO SCIENTISTS AS 'DAMP'.

Perhaps the most famous export from Wales is Tom Jones. He knew Elvis, you know, but he doesn't like to mention it. Apart from all the time.

Currency:

BRITISH POUND

While, for example, an American accent is ideally suited to barking 'The president is in danger, INITIATE THE PROTOCOLS,' the Welsh accent is optimised to say, 'Now, who'd like a slice of lovely cake?'

Capital:

CARDIFF

In the 19th century, while the English and Scottish, like the Irish, left their homelands to seek better lives overseas, the Welsh remembered that they had coal and gold and were perfectly fine at home, thanks. Also, they liked it there. That's why you never go to another country and see a Welsh bar.

Famous people:

TOM JONES, ANTHONY HOPKINS, CATHERINE ZETA-JONES, SHIRLEY BASSEY, MICHAEL SHEEN, CHARLOTTE CHURCH, ROB BRYDON

The national symbol of Wales is the dragon, but a really nice dragon that remembers to call its mum every Sunday.

BEHIND THE SCENES

Everyone's about natural, locally sourced ingredients these days. So why can't the same logic be applied to cars? In what almost counts as consumer journalism, *The Grand Tour* went to find out. In Wales.

The May mud car MkI. Note the attempt to make fake headlights out of mud. They fell off. Everything fell off.

The genuine Clarksonian and Hammondic laughter that only comes from realising James has been a spectacular clot. Again.

Left, a simple creature with hairy ears is lured towards meat. Also, a dog. His name was Pepper.

'And this is called a flower.' Country boy Hammond shares his in-depth knowledge.

You can't make a silk purse out of a cow's ear. But you can make a rear view mirror out of a cow's ear. If you must.

Above, the eco cars bring chaos and confusion to a Welsh village and then, below, to a Welsh field. Note Hammond attempting to extinguish fire with a stick, the silly man.

A rare sighting of the Lesser Spotted May, lurking within the dirty straw of his own stupid car.

Maggots on a Land Rover Discovery oil-filler cap. Not a standard feature.

When the floods come, the only things to survive will be James May, a car seat and an on-board camera.

Deleted scene: Jeremy finds his small, furry 'parts department'.

DO YOU SPEAK...

WELSH

YDYCH CHI'N SIARAD CYMRAEG?

Welsh is a fantastic language for anyone who hates vowels and thinks there are too many of them in English. But did you know Welsh is also one of the most expressive languages for describing cars and motoring? Here are some unique Welsh words for which there are no direct English equivalents.

LLYLL

Small rectangle of felt stuck to the side of a seatbelt buckle to stop it rattling against the centre console.

LLYLLYLL

A tight turn taken more gently than normal because there is a takeaway curry on the passenger seat.

LLYLLWLLYN

A low-speed accident caused by a driver becoming distracted by an attractive pedestrian wearing fewer clothes than normal because it's the first warm day of the year.

LLYLLYLLWYLLYN

The tiny, wedge-shaped block of rubber attached to the leading front-door pillar of many cars for reasons that aren't entirely clear.

LLYLLYLLYLLYLLWYLL

The softest, shortest sounding of a car horn it is humanly possible to make, used exclusively when you want to tell someone the lights have turned green without seeming rude.

LLYLLYLLYLL YLLWYLLYNWYLLN

To ignore a sat-nav instruction because you are convinced that the sat-nav is wrong.

LLYLLWYLLYNW NYNLLYWNWLLGNTH

The tiny writing at the bottom of a personalised number plate that explains what the letters and numbers on the plate are supposed to say.

LLYLLYL LYLLYLLY LLYLLYLLYLL YLLYSNGNTH

To park on the far side of the car park in the hope that no one will park next to you and ding your paintwork again, even though it means an extra 10-minute walk to the shop.

LLYLLYLL YLLYLL YLLYLLYLL YLLYWNGHTHYLLY LLYN

To say thank you to the person who has just let you out of a side turning by flashing your hazard lights precisely twice.

LLYLLYLLYLLYLLYLLYLLYLL YLLYLLYLLYLLYLLYLLLLLLL

A badly adjusted windscreen-washer jet.

WORLD'S BEST POLICE CARS
VAUXHALL ASTRA DIESEL

COUNTRY	UK
TOP SPEED	124 MPH
0-62 MPH	10.2 SECONDS

Against the rest of the world, the British police do not come out well, car-wise. Gone are the days of V8-powered Rover SDIs and wildly sliding Ford Granadas in telly cop dramas from an era when the average Brit cop smoked as much as the back tyres on his squad car. Of course, every so often they'll roll out some Lotus or Focus RS covered in day-glo Battenburg and ask us to believe that plod is proceeding in a westerly direction at 200 mph, but the truth is always something like this: a worthy diesel Vauxhall with lots of aerials on the roof, shuffling its way carefully through a housing estate while four yoofs in a stolen Golf R have already made it halfway across the next county. Frankly, it's embarrassing.

RENAULT MEGANE RS

COUNTRY	FRANCE
TOP SPEED	147 MPH
0-62 MPH	6.5 SECONDS

For the average French bobbie, work-time transport is some dreary diesel Peugeot, but some members of the Gendarmerie are a bit luckier than that because they get to thrash about the place in one of the greatest hot hatchbacks in history. For French crims this might be tremendous news since there's every chance they can pull over mid-chase, certain in the knowledge that their pursuers will zoom past and drive into the distance, simply because they're having too much fun to stop.

GRAND TOUR RENTALS

TAKE THE STRESS OUT OF YOUR LIFE AND PUT IT INTO SOMETHING MORE SPECIFIC, LIKE A VERY GENUINE CONCERN THAT YOU HAVEN'T GOT ENOUGH INSURANCE.

TO CHOOSE YOUR HIRE CAR FROM GRAND TOUR RENTALS, SIMPLY SELECT YOUR PREFERRED LOCATION.

WALES

ANIMAL-BASED 'ECO CAR'

See the natural beauty of the place where Richard Hammond almost lives from behind the unhygienic wheel of a Land Rover-based eco car, made mostly from bones and skin and flies and smell.

£140 per day. Nose tampons not included.

ITALY

DODGE CHALLENGER HELLCAT

What better way to enjoy the cultural and natural delights of Italy than from behind the wheel of an incredibly moronic car? Whether cruising through the Tuscan countryside or rolling into Florence, you're sure to appreciate the thunderous exhaust and oafish appearance of a car described by GRAND TOUR RENTALS co-founder Richard Hammond as 'brilliant', and then he did a thumbs-up.

€180 per day. Stained vest optional.

MOROCCO

ALFA ROMEO 4C

Take in the majesty of the jewel of North Africa from behind the uncomfortable and idiotically expensive wheel of a machine described by most people as 'flawed' and by GRAND TOUR RENTALS co-founder Jeremy Clarkson as 'literally the best car ever'. Wherever you stay, you're sure to cut a dash as you pull up to your hotel in this Alfa Romeo. And then tumble out of it in an undignified way because the doors are too small and the sills are too wide.

6,000 dirhams per day.

NAMIBIA

BEACH BUGGY

A beach buggy is the ideal way to see the apparently endless coast of Namibia and a less-than-ideal way in which to drive the country's incredibly bumpy roads. GRAND TOUR RENTALS is proud to offer a choice of three beach buggies from its Namibian fleet, so whether you enjoy fire damage, unreliability and petrol leaks, or simply like being suspended from a helicopter, there's sure to be something for you here.

2,500 NADs per day.

ENGLAND

THE EXCELLENT

There is so much to see in England, and you're sure to see some of it in a machine that combines all the worst parts of an off-roader with all the very terrible parts of a rusty 1980s soft-top. Created by un-renowned atelier Jeremy Clarkson, known in some circles as the idiotic Pininfarina of England, The Excellent is sure to provide you with little or no pleasure whatsoever.

£1m per day.

DUBAI

HOVERCRAFT

Dubai is the ideal destination for anyone looking to relax on a beach, dive in clear seas, jet ski into open waters or take part in any number of exciting outdoor pursuits. Why not make your all-action Dubai holiday complete by zooming wildly out of control over a shallow lake in front of a hotel, crashing into a tent and getting sucked horrifically into the intake mechanism of a small hovercraft. It's a dream that only GRAND TOUR RENTALS can make true.

1,000 AED. Clean-up not included.

FRANCE (NORTH)

MASERATI BITURBO

The north of France is very much the thinking person's south of France and is rightly famed for its climate, which is ideal for people who don't like being too hot, and for its many things to see, although we can't remember what they are. Why not make your visit to France (northern bit) complete by renting one of GRAND TOUR RENTALS' three Maserati Biturbos. Whether you want power oversteer, a troublingly terminal engine fault or weirdly wet seats, we're sure to have the car for you.

€200 per day. Breakdown cover costs extra.

VIN CLARKSON IS BACK IN

THERE'S A LINE TO CROSS
AND HE'S GOING TO CROSS IT.
JUST AS SOON AS HE'S HAD LUNCH.

'Mega shizzle,
innit mate'
TAPESTRY CONSERVATION MAGAZINE

'Bulbous'
MAXIMUM MOVIE

'Even bigger and
more breathless'
FILMGASM

THE **FAT**
AND THE
FURIOUS 2

VIN CLARKSON IN THE FAT AND THE FURIOUS 2, WITH RICHARD HAMMOND, JAMES MAY AND
PRINCESS ANNE AS PRINCESS ANNE AS TOKEN FEMALE DIRECTED BY ROCK HAMMERSMACK
PRODUCED BY CHIP FACEHAMMER KEYBOARDS BY RICK WAKEMAN

HAVE YOU CONSIDERED THE...
HOVERCRAFT?

There are lots of ways to cover big distances around the world from cars to boats to aeroplanes. But most people overlook another excellent way to travel – the hovercraft. Just look at some of the advantages of making your next long-distance trip by hovercraft:

- Able to go on land or sea
- Incredibly noisy
- Extremely hard to control
- No brakes
- Idiotic

When planning your next trip, don't forget to travel by hovercraft. The extremely noisy way to lose control and have a massive accident and/or get sucked into the mechanism!

'IT'S VERY LOUD'

'WHAT?'

PIT STOP 06

MOROCCO

FOCUS ON MOROCCO

NORTHERN EUROPE
BASICALLY EVERYTHING ABOVE THIS WRITING

SOUTHERN EUROPE
LIKE NORTHERN EUROPE, BUT NICER FOOD

MOROCCO
JEWEL IN THE SOMETHING OF SOMETHING. PROBABLY.

NORTH AFRICA
A VERY LONG WAY FROM SOUTH AFRICA

a.k.a.

MAROC (IF YOU'RE FRENCH)

The internet domain for Morocco is .ma and they can't have .mo because it's used by Macau. There is no Moroccan word for this sort of irony.

Population:

34 MILLION

A casbah, or kasbah, is a type of citadel seen across Morocco. Most feature thin leather straps to prevent items falling off shelves and out of cupboards, a precautionary measure installed in case of a visit from The Clash.

Currency:

MOROCCAN DIRHAM

Casablanca is Morocco's largest city, and also its most famous thanks to the 1942 film of the same name. To capitalise on the enduring appeal of this movie, literally everything in Casablanca has been renamed 'Rick's Café', even the hospital. It's a bloody nightmare for Yelp.

Famous people:

JEAN RENO OUT OF *LÉON*. HE WAS BORN IN MOROCCO. TRUE FACT.

The city of Fez gives its name to a distinctive type of hat popular in the region. It is twinned with the American town of Baseball Caap.

Capital:

RABAT. DON'T SAY CASABLANCA, THAT WOULD BE WRONG.

Morocco is the world's largest producer of canned sardines. As a result, the country is almost constantly being brushed against by cats.

In remote parts of the Atlas Mountains they speak of 'tawil alqammat aihmaq', which literally translates as 'tall silly man in horrible jacket driving too expensive sports car'.

BEHIND THE SCENES

What's the first place you think of when someone says 'lightweight sports cars'? If you said 'Morocco', you're right. You're also talking to a book, you weirdo. Anyway, Jeremy, Richard and James had some light cars and they went there. Just because.

As a child, the young Richard Hammond dreamt that one day he would be a real-life television presenter. He didn't realise it would involve this.

Above, a slow-moving and stubborn creature tries to control a donkey. Below, the high-speed camera-tracking car with 'Russian Arm' attachment.

Style. You've either got it. Or you're a silly man standing in Morocco in a linen suit.

Guess what this means. Go on, have a guess. What do you reckon? You'll never get it. Oh. You have. Well done.

Above, the Alfa Romeo 4C Spider demonstrates another of its many flaws – it's a bit blurry.

Left, Richard Hammond smashes a small Mazda through an old movie prop. Or, as he believes it, a 'priceless artefact'.

Above left, a rare sighting of a creature not indigenous to Morocco – the leaping Hammond.

Below, one of the crack camera people films the fake F-16 jet from *The Jewel of the Nile* movie.

MOROCCAN MOVIES

As Jeremy and James discovered when they visited Morocco, the country has its own large and successful film industry. As Richard discovered when he visited Morocco, the country has some 'ancient ruins' and a 'spaceship'. Here are some of the lesser-known movies set in Morocco.

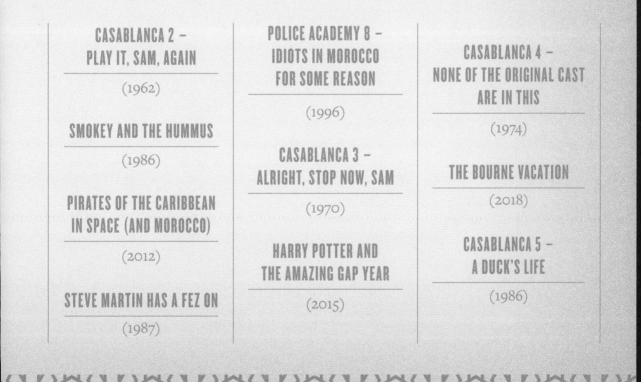

CASABLANCA 2 –
PLAY IT, SAM, AGAIN

(1962)

SMOKEY AND THE HUMMUS

(1986)

PIRATES OF THE CARIBBEAN
IN SPACE (AND MOROCCO)

(2012)

STEVE MARTIN HAS A FEZ ON

(1987)

POLICE ACADEMY 8 –
IDIOTS IN MOROCCO
FOR SOME REASON

(1996)

CASABLANCA 3 –
ALRIGHT, STOP NOW, SAM

(1970)

HARRY POTTER AND
THE AMAZING GAP YEAR

(2015)

CASABLANCA 4 –
NONE OF THE ORIGINAL CAST
ARE IN THIS

(1974)

THE BOURNE VACATION

(2018)

CASABLANCA 5 –
A DUCK'S LIFE

(1986)

AIRLINES WE HAVE LOST

There are many airlines in the world, but what about those airlines that were in the world and now are not? Well, here are some lesser-known examples of that.

Welsh-Dutch Airways (1971–1972)

Boasting just one route – Llandudno to Groningen – Welsh-Dutch Airways quickly discovered two important problems with its business model. First, there aren't many people who want to fly from North Wales to the north-eastern Netherlands. And second, there isn't an airport in Llandudno. This latter point perhaps explains the amount of damage repeatedly suffered by the undercarriage and wings of their one plane, a Hepworth-Bassingly HBH6 Super Furious, which eventually crashed into the North Sea with the loss of all seven magazines on board. Just nine months later, Welsh-Dutch Airways closed down, although it returned in 1985 as a type of anti-perspirant.

British Homeways (1974–1982)

This airline was known for its fleet of Hanbury-Wells J9 'Smokemaker' aircraft, a machine famed for producing an unusually high sound and quantity of flames. British Homeways stood apart from rivals because they recognised that a lot of British people liked the idea of flying but

didn't want to go abroad. With that in mind, BH offered flights on popular routes such as Manchester Ringway to Manchester Ringway and Leeds Bradford to Leeds Bradford. 'All the glamour of flying without the unpleasantness of going abroad!' was the company's slogan until 1982, when the airline went into administration after British people decided they probably would risk going abroad after all.

Maverick (1986–1987)

The brainchild of Floridian meat billionaire John P. Hammertime, Maverick's unique selling point was to offer affordable air travel from the UK to Orlando, while also giving passengers a sense of what it would be like to feature in the popular 1980s movie *Top Gun*. As such, all take-offs were needlessly vertical and everyone on board had to wear Aviator sunglasses. Maverick cut costs by featuring a mid-flight refuelling stop in Newfoundland, during which all passengers were forced to play a game of shirtless volleyball and then zoom about on a motorcycle while not wearing a crash helmet. Maverick existed for just 11 months before its aviation

out of business in 1979 after Nana Mouskouri appeared to say the word 'grunties' on Michael Parkinson's chat show and everyone in Britain went off Greek stuff.

Poundair (1996–1997)

Part of the 1990s explosion in budget airlines, Poundair was founded by Scottish entrepreneur Fergus Spurgeon on the very simple premise that all flights would cost a pound (plus £50 admin fee, plus £75 baggage charge, plus £100 fee if you wanted to use steps to get on the plane). Flying from Prestwick to a range of European airports 50 miles from the cities they purported to serve, Poundair

licence was withdrawn because it kept 'buzzing' the 'tower', despite being told not to.

Aviatytos (1976–1979)

In the mid-1970s Britain experienced something of a boom in Greek things. Demis Roussos was in the charts, moussaka was on the dinner table and people were taking package holidays to Greece for the first time. Athens-based Aviatytos aimed to capitalise on this by offering affordable flights

with 'an intensely Greek flavour'. This turned out to be too intense for many passengers, who claimed there were 'far too many people' on each flight and that the 'in-flight entertainment' consisted of one song that started quite slowly as the plane took off from Britain and then got faster and faster throughout the four-hour flight. Also, some customers noted that the plane didn't seem to have as much glass in the windows as they expected. Aviatytos went

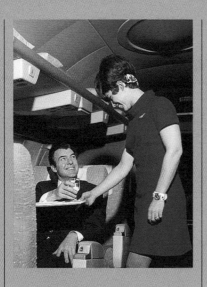

aimed to cut costs with a variety of controversial measures. These were later to prove its downfall when authorities ruled that, contra to the airline's trenchant belief, it really was obliged to provide passengers with seats, and that it had no right to save fuel by refusing to climb beyond 500 feet for the entire journey.

Zbbbbbrrrrrr (2010–2012)

An ultra-low-cost airline from Poland, Zbbbbbrrrrrr was able to offer flights from London Luton to Warsaw from as little as £4.50, based on the unusual concept that no one actually got on the plane or travelled to their destination. Instead, anyone booking a Zbbbbbrrrrrr 'flight' from the UK would receive photographs of Poland or, in the case of business travellers, receipts from hotels and restaurants, enabling them to convince friends and colleagues they had been away without the bother of leaving the house. Initially very successful, Zbbbbbrrrrrr floundered when the company remembered that, despite its ingenious no-flight business model, it actually owned an expensive fleet of 20 Russian-made Kvolliat Design Bureau KN-25 'Death Plunge' airliners. Plus, several of these planes had been involved in accidents despite being parked on the tarmac at Warsaw airport, forcing the airline to send pre-booked passengers photos of the inside of a Polish hospital.

POSTCARD

FROM THE TENT

STUTTGART

Having a great time here in Stuttgart. Except it's not strictly Stuttgart because the place we found to pitch the tent is actually in a place called Ludwigsburg which is outside Stuttgart but no one realised that until it was too late. Oh well.

Another thing we didn't discover until the night before filming was that a local politician was seriously trying to ban us from filming. Fortunately, he didn't manage it. Show went ahead, audience was brilliant, one of the best of the tour so far. Maybe even the most lively and the loudest laughing. All those German clichés you've heard are wrong. Also discovered that the tent has a very sophisticated ventilation system which circulates fresh air around the place so that the audience doesn't suffocate. Good job the tent people knew about the need to do this rather than leaving all the tent infrastructure stuff to, say, Jeremy. Reason we discovered how the ventilation system works is that someone's puffer jacket fell onto the floor and was immediately sucked into the tent air intake. Oops. Whole thing had to be shut down. All in all, a great success. Celebrated by going to a bierkeller. Think that's what it was. It was down some steps and they served beer. Hope all is well at home,

THE GRAND TOUR

WORLD'S BEST POLICE CARS
SUBARU LEGACY

COUNTRY	JAPAN
TOP SPEED	130 MPH
0-62 MPH	9.6 SECONDS

There isn't much crime in Japan, and you could imagine that when some takes place the perpetrator leaves behind a short letter of apology. As a result of operating in a relatively low-crime society, the Japanese police don't need anything fast but they spend a lot of time in their cars so they do want something pleasant. That must be why they drive Subaru Legacys. In truth, Japanese law enforcers have also been known to run Nissan 350Zs and Mazda RX8s but honestly, after a long day of paperwork you'd take the slower Subaru to the scene of the offence and hope that the criminal was still there, politely waiting to hand himself in.

SKODA OCTAVIA VRS

COUNTRY	BELGIUM
TOP SPEED	149 MPH
0-62 MPH	7.1 SECONDS

For the police of a quiet, pleasant country like Belgium it simply wouldn't do to go roaring about the place in a Ford Crown Victoria, powersliding into a *frites* stall and causing people to spill their glasses of that strange beer that comes in a big test tube and only requires half a pint to make your head fall off. No, the Belgo-cops need something reserved and subtle, but with the ability to deliver a firm smack of power if things get tasty. What they need is the Skoda Octavia vRS. And that's what they've got. Perfect.

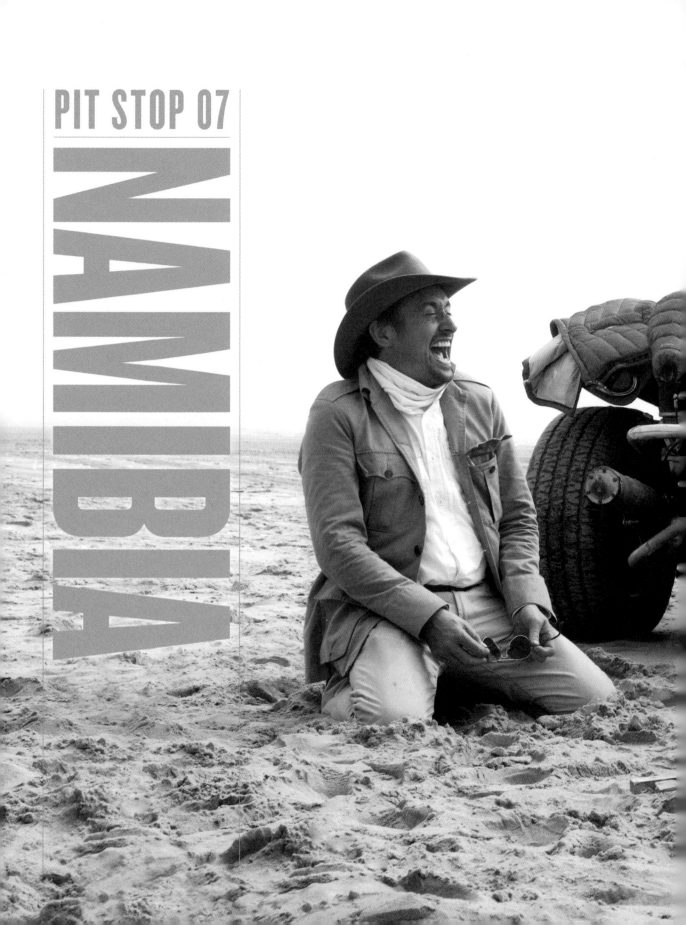

PIT STOP 07

NAMIBIA

FOCUS ON NAMIBIA

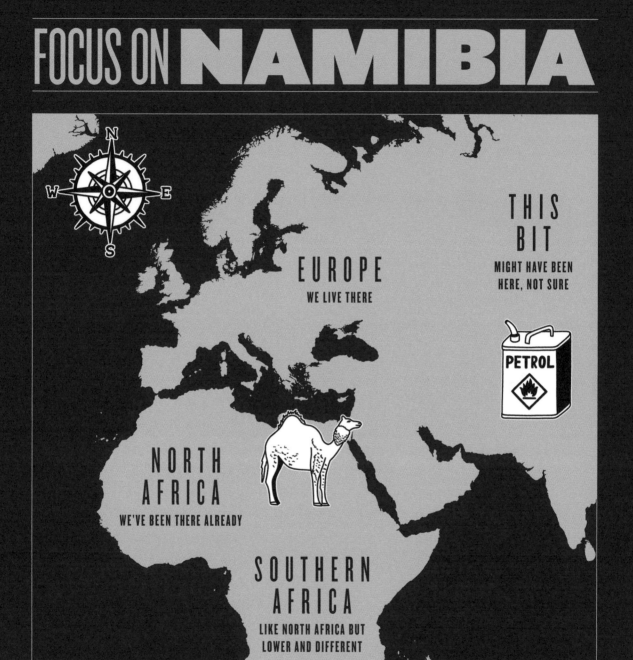

THIS BIT
MIGHT HAVE BEEN
HERE, NOT SURE

PETROL

EUROPE
WE LIVE THERE

NORTH
AFRICA
WE'VE BEEN THERE ALREADY

SOUTHERN
AFRICA
LIKE NORTH AFRICA BUT
LOWER AND DIFFERENT

NAMIBIA
IT'S ON THE RIGHT

a.k.a.

REPUBLIC OF NAMIBIA

Population:

2 MILLION

Namibia is the second-least-densely populated country on earth. Hence the local word for 'neighbour' literally translates as 'people 70 miles away'.

The Namib is thought to be the oldest desert in the world. It's also the oldest dessert in the world, being the local name for lemon meringue pie.

Famous people:

RYAN NYAMBE (FOOTBALLER), FRANKIE FREDERICKS (OLYMPIC RUNNER), HAGE GEINGOB (PRESIDENT), SHILOH NOUVEL JOLIE-PITT (ADOPTED DAUGHTER OF BRAD AND ANGELINA)

Other Namibian attractions include Fire Mountain, the Skeleton Coast and Dragon's Breath Cave. It's almost as if someone doesn't want people to go there.

Capital:

WINDHOEK

Namibia used to be run by Germans. Mind you, so did Rover and look what happened to that.

Currency:

NAMIBIAN DOLLAR

A windsock in Windhoek would make a reasonable rhyme for an Oasis song.

BEHIND THE SCENES

Beach buggies; are they rubbish, as *The Grand Tour* producer believes? Or are they great, as *The Grand Tour* presenters claim? There was only one way to sort this out. With a trip to Namibia. Obviously.

Above, a child of the sixties in a design from the sixties wearing sunglasses from the sixties. Richard Hammond, right, gives a lovely rendition of his award-winning 'unamused' face.

Above, a look inside James May's beach buggy. Note that he was so annoyed about dust in his car that he actually bought a small vacuum cleaner. What a funny man.

Right, a temporary campsite for the crew. Note James May lurking by the lavatories.

Above, Richard Hammond casually trying to disguise his 'cheating' space-frame chassis.

Below, 'Hey James, how many times has Noel Edmonds asked for that shirt back?'

Quiet, please.
Filming in progress.

Mmm.
Engine
fish.

Jeremy Clarkson, shortly after
almost being cleaved in two by
some straps.

James May,
drinking-vessel
connoisseur.

Namibia has a huge range of languages and dialects, including Oshi-wambo, Nama/Damara, Afrikaans, Kavango and Otjiherero, as well as English and German. This leads to an incredible range of unique words you will only find in this country, such as the examples below:

Taaltwatka — A badly designed beach buggy with an engine that is far too big.

Tynititka — A well-designed beach buggy that has cheated because it has a space-frame chassis.

Dullmaanka — A slow-moving beach buggy that appears to have been on fire.

Yuuwaankas — Sound made when waking up to discover your colleagues have suspended you beneath a helicopter.

Jaymsyubelund — Exclamation of surprise upon discovering that a colleague has led you in the wrong direction.

Getgeeovanee — To summon help when you literally can't be bothered to open another bottle of wine yourself.

Owmyhansfolenoff — State reached by driving all day on extremely rough roads in a beach buggy.

Hoosydeeawaziss — Frustration at realising you are stuck on a very long journey in a very inappropriate car.

Geeovaneeisbrocken — My butler seems to have had a horrible parasailing accident.

Ohhfukifuk — Sound made when you appear to be stuck over a crocodile-infested river.

POSTCARD
FROM THE TENT

Made it to Dubai for the last recording of Series 1. Lost Jeremy and James in the airport on the way here, then found them again, happy as anything sitting in what appeared to be someone's living room.

Staying in a hotel that must be very fashionable because it's quite dark inside. Also, it has fashionably complicated showers that lure you into the cubicle and then make freezing water pour out of what you thought was the light fitting. At least, that's what happened to Jeremy. Recording went really well, apart from a slight hovercraft mishap that we won't bore you with here. Afterwards, the whole team assembled to watch the massive Burj Khalifa building light up with a huge Grand Tour light show featuring moving cars and the presenters' faces and all sorts. Except the place where we assembled was on a balcony at the bottom of the building which turned out to be literally the worst place possible to see the actual display. We're a very organised show. Looking forward to coming home soon,

THE GRAND TOUR

THE PERFECT HOLIDAY

WITH RICHARD HAMMOND

The star of *Richard Hammond's Wild Weather*, *Richard Hammond's Eye Surgery Mishaps* and *Richard Hammond's When Animals Fall Over* invites us into his luxurious broken Land Rover storage barn to talk us through his perfect holiday, and reveals how *you* can have the same experience.

The hallowed turf of the camping-supplies shop. Happy times.

'The thing about going abroad is that it's quite far away,' observes TV's Richard Hammond, relaxing in a tatty car seat on the floor of his palatial draughty barn, almost in Wales. 'That's why my ideal holiday is going to the English Lake District and sleeping in a tent.'

'I don't know what it is about two weeks' camping in the Lake District that appeals to me so much,' the star continues, idly fiddling with a rusted alternator mounting. 'I suppose it's a combination of many things, such as damp and cold and more damp. Lovely.'

Richard clearly recognises that not everyone is in the lucky position of being able to pop to the Lake District whenever they feel like it, so he kindly agreed to share some tips on getting that camping-in-the-Lakes feeling, even if you live elsewhere in the world…

ACCOMMODATION

'It has to be a tent,' says Richard. 'And ideally one that's quite small. I love the cosiness of a tiny tent and the luxurious feeling of attempting to put on or remove your trousers while lying down. You don't have to do that in a five-star hotel, do you? I suppose you could anyway, but it'd be a bit weird.'

LOCATION

'It's vital to pitch your tent in the right place,' Richard explains. 'If you live somewhere dry, remember to soak the ground with gallons of water and sheep wee before you set up, and do take account of the prevailing wind, of which there should be lots. You won't be getting the full experience if you're not tucked up inside a sleeping bag at night, listening to a howling gale attempting to rip the roof from over your head and dash it into a slurry pit in the valley below.'

ACTIVITIES

'Walking. That's what you do in the Lakes,' Richard says carefully. 'Strolling the tree-lined streets of a fashionable European city before returning to a boutique hotel is all well and good, but you can't beat the feeling of trudging for 20 miles up and down mountains and then returning all cold and wet to the place where your tent used to be. Also, if the weather is too nice to go walking, in the Lakes you can always visit the Pencil Museum in Keswick, so if you can't make it to this area, stay wherever you are but have a look at some pencils.'

'... damp and cold and more damp. Lovely'

Almost perfect, if only there were more drizzle. And owls.

DINING

'I never understand why people get so excited about Michelin-starred restaurants,' Richard muses. 'What's wrong with a tin of beans cooked over a tiny camping stove that keeps going out because it's so windy? You can sing the praises of fancy food like salad or chicken kiev but for my money you can't beat a tin plate of lukewarm beans'.

CLOTHING

'I hear people saying, "Oooh, I must get my holiday wardrobe ready," and I think, what's the point?' Richard observes. 'If you want the full Lakes experience, just ask yourself this: Is it thick and is it waterproof? Also, does every single thing I'm wearing make a rustling sound? Perfect.'

PEOPLE WE HAVE LOST

The world is a wonderful and exciting place, but it can also be a dangerous one, as tragically illustrated by the number of high-quality celebrities who passed away during the first series of globe-straddling kind-of-a-car-programme *The Grand Tour*. Here we remember those who were lost:

JEREMY RENNER
(1971–2016)

ACTOR, SINGER, PARACHUTIST, DEPTH-PERCEPTION ERROR-MAKER

ARMIE HAMMER
(1986–2016)

ACTOR, DESERT STROLLER, SNAKE BAIT

CHARLIZE THERON
(1975–2016)

ACTOR, PRODUCER, LION LUNCH

JIMMY CARR
(1972–2016)

COMEDIAN, PRESENTER, JET-SKI DEVOTEE, RED PUDDLE

GOLDEN EARRING
(FORMED 1961, TRANSFORMED 2016)

BARRY HAY, RINUS GERRITSEN, GEORGE KOOYMANS, CESAR ZUIDERWIJK, AAL DJEAD

CAROL VORDERMAN
(1960–2016)

BROADCASTER, WRITER, MATHS DOER, UNEXPLAINED EXPIRATION ENTHUSIAST

KIMI RAIKKONEN
(1979–2016)

RACING DRIVER, BOOZE FAN, UNSETTLING BUMP IN THE SNOW

NENA
(1960–2016)

SINGER, SONGWRITER, HIGH-ALTITUDE BURSTING PERSON

SIR CHRIS HOY
(1976–2016)

CYCLIST, RACING DRIVER, SCOTCH MIST

BRIAN JOHNSON
(1947–2016)

SINGER, SONGWRITER, RACER, PANCAKE

DANIEL RICCIARDO
(1989–2016)

RACING DRIVER, SMILING FAN, TENT STAIN

TIM BURTON
(1958–2016)

DIRECTOR, PRODUCER, WRITER, MONSTER MEAT

SIMON PEGG
(1970–2016)

ACTOR, WRITER, PRODUCER, SEAGULL ATTRACTION

IMPORTANT NOTE: IT HAS BEEN BROUGHT TO OUR ATTENTION THAT THESE PEOPLE ARE IN FACT NOT DEAD. REPEAT, NOT DEAD. SORRY.

WORLD'S BEST POLICE CARS

FORD CROWN VICTORIA

COUNTRY	USA
TOP SPEED	128 MPH
0-62 MPH	8.9 SECONDS

In many ways the definitive police car, not for its performance or its sterling record of bringing down crims, but because it's appeared in hundreds of movies and TV shows, thundering about the place in a cloud of V8 fury and long, lurid power slides. Sadly, the Crown Vic ceased production in 2011, to be replaced by a variety of new police models, many of which had V6 engines and four-wheel drive and were therefore better at chasing bad guys but much worse at doing it in a cool way.

A HORSE

COUNTRY	CANADA
TOP SPEED	NOT MUCH
0-62 MPH	TRICKY

The Canadians call them the mounted police because each officer is mounted on one of these: a horse. No, it isn't fast nor does it have good handling but, on the plus side, it doesn't need petrol, it can be persuaded to expand the law-enforcement fleet at almost no expense and it can be trained to make a woo-woo-woo sound on command. Probably. Do Canadian police also have cars? We simply don't know. But given that Canada is literally the most pleasant country in the world and probably doesn't have any crime as a result, it's doubtful that they need them. All they need is carrots and sugar lumps. And a police-branded shovel.

PIT STOP 08

GERMANY

& AUSTRIA

FOCUS ON GERMANY & AUSTRIA

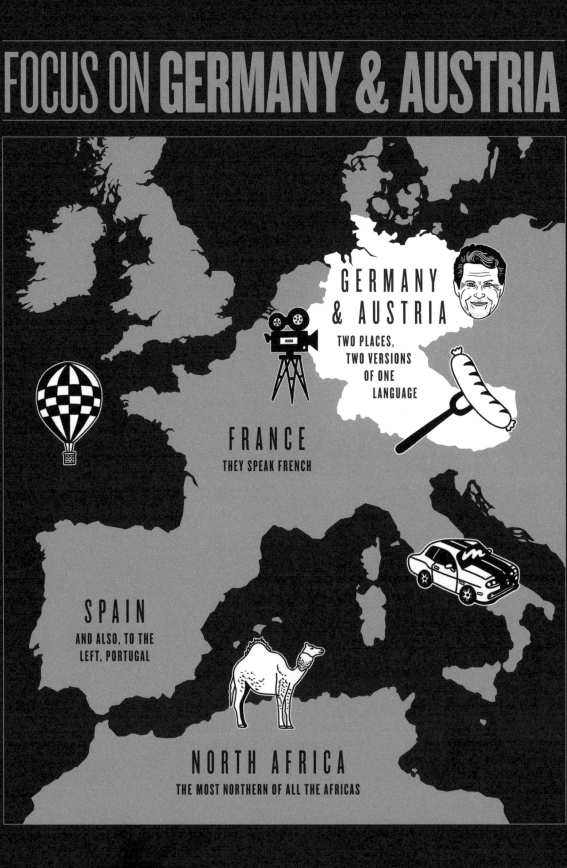

GERMANY & AUSTRIA

TWO PLACES, TWO VERSIONS OF ONE LANGUAGE

FRANCE

THEY SPEAK FRENCH

SPAIN

AND ALSO, TO THE LEFT, PORTUGAL

NORTH AFRICA

THE MOST NORTHERN OF ALL THE AFRICAS

DEUTSCHLAND UND ÖSTERREICH

a.k.a.

German wedding vows contain two extra paragraphs about neatness.

Population:

82 MILLION (GERMANY)

9 MILLION (AUSTRIA)

Austria has very stringent noise laws and if Julie Andrews really were to make the 'hills' come 'alive' with the 'sound of music' she would be arrested immediately.

Capital: (Germany)

BERLIN

Capital: (Austria)

VIENNA

Germans love meat, bread and beer. Frankly it's a miracle the whole place doesn't stink.

German contains many long words such as *Dieschandezweiminutenfüreintreffenzuseindasnichtvongroßerbedeutungist* which is the word for the feeling of shame brought on by being two minutes late for a not-very-important meeting.

Currency:

EURO

62 per cent of Austria is on a hill.

Famous people from Germany:

MICHAEL SCHUMACHER, SEBASTIAN VETTEL, HEIDI KLUM, BORIS BECKER, CLAUDIA SCHIFFER, LUDWIG VAN BEETHOVEN

Famous people from Austria:

NIKI LAUDA, TOTO WOLFF, ARNOLD SCHWARZENEGGER, SIGMUND FREUD, FELIX BAUMGARTNER, WOLFGANG AMADEUS MOZART

Famous people who, rather neatly for the purposes of this discussion, can claim to be both German and Austrian:

CHRISTOPH WALTZ

Austria is one of the world's greatest nations for recycling. Funnily enough, Ferdinand Porsche was Austrian and he invented the 911.

BEHIND THE SCENES

Got an argument you need to resolve? Quick, let's go to Germany and Austria said no one ever. Except *The Grand Tour*, who went there to find the best high-riding 4x4 thing. Although Jeremy said he knew the answer in advance. So no change there then.

The majesty of a Range Rover in full flight, poised to give rival cars a damn good Güterweg.

Güterweg
Fucking

Above, Jeremy Clarkson steps out with an invisible lady.

'Look, James, beans.'
'Look, Jeremy, I'm not interested.'

The *Grand Tour* camera crew get some scene-setting establishing shots before a drag race. Then they move out of the way, otherwise they'll be run over.

GERMAN SPECIAL EDITIONS

Mullets! Moustaches! Salmon-coloured smart-casual jackets! In many ways Germany follows its own path when it comes to taste, and that includes the special-edition versions of their cars. While the stuff they sell to the rest of the world is simple and ungimmicky, at home they cut loose with limited-production cars to suit local tastes. Here are some highlights.

**Audi 100
Benny Hill Edition** (1985)

VW Golf Hasselhoff (1989)

BMW 535i M People (1993)

VW Polo Hasselhoff (1997)

Audi A4 Turdyparty (2000)

VW Passat Hasselhoff (2002)

**Mercedes C63 AMG
Ralf Schumacher Edition** (2009)

VW Golf Hasselhoff (2012)

Porsche 911 Mistress (2014)

**Mercedes S600 Maybach
Sexy Trouser** (2017)

THE GRAND TOUR'S
EBOLADROME

SUBSTATION
Turn hard here or end up in some electricity.

OLD LADY'S HOUSE
A chicane located by an old lady's house. She says she likes cars. She even used to have one.

FIELD OF SHEEP
Another hard left turn or you'll skid into some lamb chops.

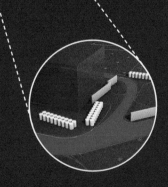

START/FINISH LINE
Where things begin and, hopefully, end.

THERE ARE MANY TRACKS IN THE WORLD, BUT ONLY ONE OF THEM LOOKS LIKE A HORRENDOUS HAEMORRHAGIC FEVER VIRUS. AT LEAST, AS FAR AS WE KNOW. THAT PLACE IS THE GRAND TOUR'S EXCLUSIVE TEST TRACK WHERE CARS CAN BE PUSHED TO THE LIMIT WITH ALMOST NO RISK OF CLATTERING THROUGH AN OLD LADY'S FRONT WINDOW. IT'S FAST, IT'S CHALLENGING AND ITS LOCATION IS ABSOLUTELY TOP SECRET. UNLESS YOU DO A QUICK SEARCH FOR IT ON THE INTERNET.

YOUR NAME HERE CORNER
Sponsorship opportunities are still available so please do get in touch.

ISN'T STRAIGHT
It's a straight that isn't. Features a super-fast left, then two rights. Other features include lots of wildlife, many trees and no run-off areas. Gulp.

THE GRAND TOUR'S
SWIND-O-FACTS!

100% TRUE AT TIME OF PRINT

THE *GRAND TOUR* TEST TRACK IS LOCATED IN A TOP-SECRET LOCATION THAT CANNOT BE DISCLOSED, ALTHOUGH WE CAN REVEAL THAT IT'S NEAR THE BRITISH TOWN OF SWINDON. BUT WHAT IS A SWINDON? WELL, HERE ARE SOME COMPLETELY GENUINE SWIND-O-FACTS TO BRING YOU UP TO SPEED.

SCRATCHINGS

Swindon's name is thought to derive from the Old English for 'pig hill'.

FRISKY

In the early 2000s Swindon was described as 'the teenage pregnancy capital of Britain'.

STEAMY

Isambard Kingdom Brunel built a huge railway works in Swindon. It's since been knocked down.

BUFFERING

In 2007 Swindon had the UK's highest level of broadband access.

ACTORING

Billie Piper is from Swindon.

PAMPLEMOUSSE

Swindon used to be home to a large Renault logistics centre.

CHUNKY

Seventy per cent of people in Swindon are classed as overweight or obese.

ROTARY

Swindon is most famous for having a complicated roundabout.

BITS

Swindon is home to a small museum of computing.

AROUND THE WORLD

WITH THE AMERICAN

Never popular *Grand Tour* character The American has been all over the world, usually against his will. Here he gives his analysis of some popular places around the globe. Don't worry, you won't hear from him again after this.

LONDON

'DRIVE ON THE WRONG SIDE, BEER ALL BROWN, UNDERSTAND ABOUT 20 PER CENT OF WHAT THEY'RE SAYING. DON'T BOTHER.'

PARIS

'WELL, EXCUSE ME, MR FANCY PANTS, IT'S CALLED A GODDAMN BURGER IN MY COUNTRY AND WE SAVED YOUR ASSES IN WORLD WAR 2.'

RIO DE JANEIRO

'I SAW A LADY WITH A SWIMMING COSTUME THAT WAS RIGHT UP HER BUTT. BUT COULD I ORDER A BURGER AND FRIES? COULD I HELL. TERRIBLE.'

SAN FRANCISCO

'YEAH, IT'S THE US, BUT FANCY PANTS US. TAKE YOUR CRAFT BEER AND SHOVE IT, HIPSTER.'

SANTIAGO

'SEE, I LIKE CHILLI WHEN IT'S SERVED ON A HOT DOG. I DIDN'T KNOW IT'S ALSO A DAMN PLACE. NO THANK YOU, SIR.'

SYDNEY

'YEAH, REAL FRIENDLY PEOPLE, BUT THEY DRIVE ON THE WRONG DAMN SIDE OF THE ROAD. ASK ME HOW I FOUND THAT OUT. ACTUALLY DON'T.'

TORONTO

'YOU WANNA GO TO AN AMERICA WHERE THEY TALK STRANGE AND EAT WEIRD STUFF AND GET REAL FUNNY IF YOU GET YOUR GUN OUT? FINE, BE MY GUEST.'

ATHENS

'SEE, IF WE HAD ONE OF THOSE OLDEST BUILDINGS IN THE WORLD IN AMERICA YOU CAN SURE AS SHIT BET WE WOULDN'T HAVE LET IT GET IN THAT CONDITION. HUH.'

STOCKHOLM

'IT'S TOO DAMN COLD AND THE BEER'S TOO DAMN EXPENSIVE. NEXT. NO WAIT. ALSO VOLVOS CAN SUCK MY ASS.'

MOSCOW

'MY DADDY DIDN'T FIRE A GUN AT THE TV IN THE '70s FOR GODDAMN COMMUNISM TO WIN. NO, SIR.'

JAPAN

'WHO IN HELL WANTS TO GO OUT FOR A BEER AND SING TO HIS FRIENDS? WEIRDOS, THAT'S WHO. GODDAMN WEIRDOS.'

MUNICH

'OH SURE, THEY HAVE BEER. BUT THEN THEY SERVE IT WITH SAUSAGE AND CURRY SHIT. AND THEY DON'T DONE SPEAK ENGLISH RIGHT NEITHER.'

KOREA

'SO YOU GOT THE NUKEY GUY IN THE TOP HALF, AND THE OTHER GUYS IN THE BOTTOM HALF. I THINK THEY MADE MY TV.'

HANOI

'MY DADDY FOUGHT THESE GUYS. IT WAS A LOCAL ZONING PERMIT DISPUTE IN THE '80s BUT THAT AIN'T THE POINT. I STILL AIN'T FORGOTTEN.'

CAPE TOWN

'THOUGHT THIS SOUNDED KINDA FUN, LIKE BATMAN OR SOMETHING. NOT AT ALL. AND THEY KINDA TALK ENGLISH, BUT IN A STOOPID WAY.'

DUBAI

'ALL THESE GUYS WANDERING AROUND IN WHITE ROBES. I THOUGHT I WAS BEING CHASED BY GHOSTS. NOT FOR ME.'

MUMBAI

'WHICH DAMN SIDE OF THE ROAD ARE YOU GUYS DRIVIN' ON? DON'T ANSWER, I'M LEAVIN'.'

GIZA

'IF I WANTED TO SEE A DAMN PYRAMID, I'D GO TO VEGAS. AND WHAT IN HECKNATION IS A SPINX ANYWAYS?'

BEIJING

'CHINESE AIN'T A PEOPLE, IT'S A FOOD. BUT IT'S ALSO A PEOPLE.'

PORT MORESBY

'PAPUA NEW GUINEA? GET OUTTA HERE. THAT AIN'T A PLACE, THAT'S LIKE SOME ENGLISH GUY ASKING HIS DADDY FOR MONEY. WHAT? IT IS A PLACE? SHEESH. SEE, THIS IS WHY THE WORLD IS FREAKIN' WEIRD AND YOU'RE BETTER OFF STAYIN' HOME.'

3 MINUTES WITH ...

JAMES MAY

A rapid-fire Q&A with the ex-magazine sub-editor turned *Grand Tour* presenter.

WE'VE ONLY GOT 10 SECONDS LEFT

HELLO, JAMES.

Hello.

So, first question …
Just to clarify, the idea for this feature is that you have precisely three minutes of my time and must ask as many questions as possible?

Yes, that's right.
How are you timing it?

On my phone. Look.
Ah, yes. They're pretty accurate, the clocks in mobile phones. I'm talking about the actual clocks, of course, but the stopwatch is a component of that. Most of them regularly synchronise with a server that will itself take time from a highly accurate timekeeping device, probably an atomic clock, which of course is very precise, though not unerringly so since there are various other factors at work, and frequently the chips in everyday devices contain offsets or 'cheats' in order to compensate for other factors.

Yes, so anyway …
But when it comes to watches, it's ironic that you can spend thousands on an exquisitely made mechanical watch and yet it will be less accurate than a five quid digital bought from a petrol station.

Yes, I see, but …
Really, it's one of the greatest achievements of modern mankind that you can, for relatively little money, buy a device that is so fantastically accurate when it comes to timekeeping. One of the greatest breakthroughs was being able to regulate quartz in a digital way rather than having to trim the quartz tuning fork. Nowadays the chip within the watch allows for the crystal itself running 'fast', as it were, and skips crystal cycles at set intervals to allow for this. It's very clever, and the end result is that you could keep pretty accurate time for less than the price of a big sandwich.

Fascinating, but I wonder if we could get back to …
Though I suppose in some ways that's also a reflection on the price of sandwiches. If there was some kind of meal deal going on, you might be better off with the sandwich, and they'd probably throw

in a bag of crisps and a bottle of fizzy drink for the price. It's actually not bad value, except that you can't tell the time on a sandwich. Or a bag of crisps. Or a bottle of pop. And what bothers me about the meal deal is that maybe I don't want the crisps that are included, maybe I want a different sort that aren't, but then the people in the shop can get very confused. It's almost like they don't want deviation from the meal deal. You have to wonder, why are they so wedded to the meal deal? I think they're hiding something. They've over-ordered on certain things and now they're trying to get rid of them. Well, I'm onto them and I won't play that game. It's why I never do the meal deal.

I see, I just wonder if we could …
Now, if they gave away a small, cheap digital watch with the meal deal, then I might be interested because to my mind that would represent good value when you consider what you're actually getting for your four or five pounds. All that precise engineering, but very carefully designed and evolved over many years to allow mass manufacture at an accuracy that once upon a time we could only have dreamt of.

James, I was hoping we could …
The only problem is, you can't eat a small, highly accurate digital watch. You could try, but I really wouldn't. The battery isn't very good for you. Also, you might choke on the strap. Oh dear.

What?
We've only got 10 seconds left.

Well, I think we could start again, since I haven't asked any questions.
But that would defeat the purpose of this feature. Once the three minutes is up I can't speak to you anymore. It would be dishonest.

Yes, but it's not really a hard and fast rule so, if I can, I'd like to ask a few questions.

James?

Are you not speaking to me because the three minutes is up?

Really?

James May, thank you.

POSTCARD

Greetings from NASHVILLE TENNESSEE

FROM THE TENT

Having a great time here in Nashville. Got here a day early to settle in and decided to go for a walk into town. After two minutes Jeremy declared that he 'hates walking' and that we had already covered 'a million miles'.

It was actually about 200 yards. When he stopped moaning about how his 'knees are literally going to fall off' we found a place for lunch and discovered that in Tennessee 'hot chicken' refers to the spiciness and not the temperature, but only after our eyes had started bleeding. Later we met Brian Johnson out of AC/DC and went to another restaurant which was quite fashionable and we knew it was quite fashionable because it was almost pitch black inside and everyone had to use their phone torches to read the

menus. Up bright and early this morning because *The Grand Tour* is brilliantly organised and we only realised yesterday that the tent was facing a very reflective river and also the exact spot where the sun started setting, both of which made the whole set unfilmable after about 11 a.m. So we started early. Problem solved. Whole thing went very, very well. American audiences are great. Hope all good at home,

THE GRAND TOUR

P.S. Brian died.

Richard, it's Steve the broker. Are you still wanting to cancel your accident insurance?
Yep, cancel away, please. Can't really see the need.
Are you sure?
Ohhhh yes.

BARBADOS

FOCUS ON BARBADOS

NORTH AMERICA
THE AMERICA OF THE NORTH

BARBADOS
JEWEL OF THIS BIT OF THE SEA

SOUTH AMERICA
AS ABOVE BUT DOWN HERE

a.k.a.

BIM

Excellent 1980s hip-hoppist Grandmaster Flash was born in Barbados. Contrary to popular belief, the refrain in his hit 'The Message' about being close to the edge was written about an experience on an uncommonly narrow jetty.

Population:

300, 000

The national dish of Barbados is flying fish or, for kids, flying fish fingers.

Currency:

BARBADIAN DOLLAR

If you're visiting Barbados around Christmas time remember your camera and binoculars as the island attracts vast flocks of British celebrities.

Famous people:

RIHANNA, GRANDMASTER FLASH, SIR GARFIELD SOBERS, GLADSTONE SMALL

Barbados is the birthplace of rum. Shaggers nightclub in Runcorn 2-for-1 night, girls come in free, is where it goes to die.

Capital:

BRIDGETOWN

Rihanna is from Barbados. Her song 'Pon de Replay' was written after watching an episode of *Match of the Day*. Probably.

Like London, Bridgetown has a statue of Lord Nelson. But, unlike London, it's not covered in drizzle and pigeon poo.

BEHIND THE SCENES

The Grand Tour decided to do something useful for the planet by creating a coral reef in Barbados and in no way was this just an excuse for a holiday. It's funny, you never find marine biologists in cold, grey places, do you?

This man is a witch and must be burned. Although he's all wet and it'll take ages.

This was once someone's pride and joy. But it was also a Vauxhall Corsa so, you know, no harm done.

During a break in filming, Jeremy recounts a recent visit to the proctologist.

'And when we pull on this bit of rope, it makes the bearded one yawn.'

When James went diving, Jeremy and Richard had some 'exotic' cigarette smoke blown down his air pipe. Mr Wilman cut out this scene.

RIHANNA SONG EXCLUSIVE

Shortly after Jeremy, Richard and James visited Barbados, an unreleased track by popular Bajan songstress Rihanna was leaked online. Were the lyrics inspired by events she witnessed on her home island? You be the judge.

HERE THEY COME BOY
STANDIN' ON THE QUAY
HERE THEY COME BOY
CARS FALLEN IN THE SEA

HERE THEY COME BOY
GOT TO DO IT SOMEHOW
HERE THEY COME BOY
DULL ONE GOT A CRANE NOW

HERE THEY COME BOY
LITTLE ONE IS SWIMMIN'
HERE THEY COME BOY
IN A STYLE LIKE OLD WOMEN

HERE THEY COME BOY
TALL ONE HAS A NEW SHIP
HERE THEY COME BOY
WHY ARE THEY ALL SO [HEY!]

[MIDDLE 8]
THEY COME TO THE ISLAND
SEE THEM GO, SEE THEM
SMILIN'
BUT THEY DON'T KNOW
WHAT THEY DOIN'
AND THEY LOOK TERRIBLE IN
SHO ... SHO ... SHORTS

HERE THEY COME BOY
NOW THEY ON THE BEACH
HERE THEY COME BOY
SOMEONE CALL POLICE

HERE THEY COME BOY
JUST GOT THE LAND ROVER
HERE THEY COME BOY
IS THIS STORY NEARLY
OVER?

HERE THEY COME BOY
SINK IT IN THE SEA
HERE THEY COME BOY
THIS IS QUITE SILLY

HERE THEY COME BOY
CORAL GROW IN THE BLISS
HERE THEY COME BOY
WHAT WAS THE POINT OF
THIS?

OOOH MARINE BIOLOGY
DONE BY IDIOTS
OOOH MARINE BIOLOGY
DONE WHILE ON HOLIDAY
[FADE]

CLARKSON'S CAR AUCTIONS

CLARKSON'S CAR AUCTIONS IS DELIGHTED TO ANNOUNCE A FORTHCOMING LOT OF THE UTMOST DESIRABILITY AND RARITY.

Hand-crafted by a renowned British atelier, The Excellent sympathetically marries the chassis of the esteemed Land Rover Discovery in sought-after Mark I specification to the body of a Mercedes SL in the so-called 'Dallas' shape, rightly regarded as an exemplar of understated style.

Benefitting from the revered 3.9-litre V8 engine, originally by Buick of the United States and substantially improved by the Rover company of Solihull, The Excellent boasts effortless on-road performance, while the subtle but ingenious application of a Birmingham-engineered separate chassis and four-wheel-drive system promises enviable ability on more demanding terrain.

Cosmetically, the exterior of The Excellent is in exceptional order and resplendent in a grey colour from the Mazda company of Japan. This car exudes good taste, as indeed does its creator.

Conversely, the interior would benefit from some minor attention, but its hard-working condition in no way compromises the great joy this very special machine brings to any right-thinking occupant.

The Excellent represents a unique opportunity to acquire an exquisite piece of forward-thinking design and engineering, and one that is sure to become a landmark in the evolution of the automobile.

RESERVE PRICE:
£120,000

CLARKSON'S CAR AUCTIONS
'It's literally just an excuse for me to have a massive hammer'

JAMES MAY'S

HOME OR ABROAD

The Abroad is a marvellous place, full of interesting sights and sounds and people. But it's also quite far away, and getting there involves a lot of fuss with passports and airports and remembering to pack the kind of clothes you don't normally wear. Sometimes it would just be a lot easier to stay at home, where you know all the people, you don't need to remember your passport in order to move about, the temperature is what you're used to, you can wear your normal clothes and you know where everything is.

THE ABROAD	HOME	VERDICT
The Great Pyramid of Giza, Egypt Oldest and most intact of the Seven Wonders of the World, giving a fascinating insight into the achievements of an earlier civilisation.	**Home** Know where keys are. Pub is just round corner.	HOME
The Great Barrier Reef, Australia World's largest coral reef and the single biggest structure made by living organisms, covering over 130,000 square miles and home to an incredible range of marine life.	**Home** Dry, not too hot, could pop out for last orders if you fancied it.	HOME
The Grand Canyon, USA Epic 277-mile-long, mile-deep testament to the power of nature and of mankind's smallness in the general scheme of things.	**Home** A manageable size and little risk of falling to certain death. They've got a new dartboard in the pub, by the way.	HOME
The Great Wall of China Fascinating ancient fortification extending over 13,000 miles and giving a compelling insight into Chinese socio-political evolution.	**Home** Necessitates no travel whatsoever. And they've got some new crisps in the pub. There's a sort of mustard flavour that's nice.	HOME
Machu Picchu, Peru Fifteenth-century Inca citadel providing awe-inspiring insight into an ancient civilisation in breathtaking surroundings.	**Home** Much less walking, even if you have a big staircase. What's more, there's a quiz on at the pub tonight. I think Bob said he was going.	HOME
The Taj Mahal, India Intricate and iconic mausoleum on the banks of the River Yamuna, rightly famed for its beauty and majesty.	**Home** Also the name of a very excellent curry restaurant near your house. We could go there after the pub.	HOME
The Colosseum, Italy Largest amphitheatre in history and a potent symbol of the power and endurance of the Roman Empire.	**Home** Nowhere near as dusty. And much closer to the pub, which is where we should go now once you've shut up about bloody holidays again.	HOME

POSTCARD
FROM THE TENT

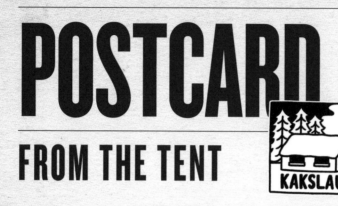

KAKSLAUTTANEN

Hello from Finland, which is very snowy. But only just. Three days ago there was no snow at all, which was looking like a bit of a problem since we were coming here to film our winter wonderland show for Christmas.

Then the first flurries of the year arrived and saved us from presenting a festive show from a drab, damp, unsnowy wood. Our international producer was so excited about the snow arriving that he decided to celebrate by misjudging a low-speed bend on the road to the hotel and tipping his hire car onto its side. Fortunately, this isn't the kind of thing that Jeremy, Richard and James would mercilessly mock him for. Um ... Filming went well, although the specially built festive Christmas grotto area of the tent got a bit smashed up, Jeremy fell over and at one point the audience was terrorised by Bob Geldof's face on a robotic tablet zooming about the tent shouting, 'What the fock is going on?' That bit will probably get cut. In other news, reindeer burgers are delicious. Happy Christmas,

THE GRAND TOUR

RALLY ROUND FINLAND

Finland has given the world some of its greatest rally drivers.
Or it might just be all the same bloke using basically anagrams
of the same name. We're not sure. Anyway, here are some fast
Finns you might not have heard of.

KAKI HOVANEN
Junior R2 champion

KIKI LOVENEN
Senior R2 champion

**WINKI
PANTONANTONEN**

N2 R1 GT2000 national
world champion

**DINKI
DONKONONKONEN**

Senior N1 K-2000 F3
international runner-up

NIKI NOVENENEN

Senior Group N junior
champion

PANTI WANKOWONKONEN

Junior senior K1 to N4 national global
running-up champion

LOVI NOVONOVONEN

R-GT senior deputy junior world
champion

LIKI VOVOVENEN

R1 junior 2000 senior national
champion (international)

TRAVEL TIPS

TENT

The idea for *The Grand Tour* tent came to Jeremy one evening while watching an episode of *True Detective* that featured a travelling preacher and his moveable church tent. What if, Clarkson thought, we had something similar for our studio? That way, rather than ask people to come to us, we could go to them.

Of course, to make this possible you can't just pop down to your local camping shop and buy a massive tent capable of accommodating cameras, a stage and a few hundred audience members. Yes, there are those big marquees used for weddings and such like but they're not designed to be used as TV studios and lack a ventilation system to make sure everyone inside doesn't suffocate, a toughened floor that's capable of taking the weight of a car and an upper structure able to withstand the sizeable load imposed by many rows of powerful lights. The only answer was to have a bespoke tent made from scratch. Or rather, two identical tents, since for logistical reasons one would leapfrog the other as the travelling circus made its way around the world.

The end result is a masterpiece made up of 723 individual parts, not one of which can be over four metres long or it won't fit in a standard shipping case. On top of that basic structure, the tent is then garnished with 1,980 pieces of lighting and electrical equipment, 829 pieces of camera and technical gear,

151 individual interior components including the floor and furniture, 170 bits of set dressing and one unconvincing fake parrot. Little wonder the whole shebang takes eight whole days to put up and requires a crew of 114 to build and run. It's also no surprise to learn that the entire set-up weighs in at a chunky 48 tonnes, which rather affects where it can go. Incidentally, taking it down demands another three days and a lot of careful re-boxing of the kind James May would admire and Jeremy Clarkson would find unimaginably tedious.

Of course, all those parts don't just make up the main studio tent. There are also surrounding support tents containing a production office, catering, a place for the presenters to get changed, and an impressive 'mission control' centre in which the director and other technical staff sit during recording. Given the ultra-high resolution of the 4K cameras and the unique travel requirements of the show, no off-the-shelf server was up to the task and a bespoke rig had to be made to deal with the unique demands of actually recording *The Grand Tour*. Oh, and for some reason the ancillary tents are all made from a special NATO-spec material that's claimed to make them invisible to radar, but the main tent is not. So that'll be the one that takes the air strike first.

All in all, the tent is a mammoth piece of design and engineering, stemming entirely from an idle thought Jeremy had at home one evening. The only bit of his plan that didn't quite work was his mistaken belief that, compared with a normal studio, a travelling tent would be cheaper and easier.

The tent is a masterpiece made up of 723 individual parts, 1,980 pieces of lighting and electrical equipment, 829 pieces of camera and technical gear and one unconvincing fake parrot.

VIN CLARKSON IS STRETCHING IT TO THE LIMITS IN

THE **FAT** AND THE **FURIOUS** 3

ONE MAN ... AND ACTUALLY TWO OTHER MEN, BUT I WANTED A POSTER THAT SAID 'ONE MAN' ON IT.

'Clarkson is bigger and more irritable than ever'
FILMGASM

'Wobbles along'
ULTRACINEMA

'Proper mental and shit'
AMATEUR POTTER MAGAZINE

**PRINCESS ANNE PRESENTS VIN CLARKSON IN THE FAT AND THE FURIOUS 3
RICHARD HAMMOND, JAMES MAY AND THAT WOMAN OUT OF THAT OTHER THING AS TOKEN FEMALE
DIRECTED BY TRENT THRUSTHAMMER PRODUCED BY KENT EAGLEHAMMER MUSIC BY ROG PROCK**

HAVE YOU CONSIDERED THE...
EKRANOPLAN ?

There are lots of ways to cover big distances around the world, from cars to boats to aeroplanes. But most people overlook another excellent way to travel – the ekranoplan. Invented by the Soviets as a top secret way to move troops and things, a massive plane that can't take off properly has many advantages:

- Achieves high speeds over water
- Can't go over any sort of land
- Noisy and a bit splashy
- High possibility of smacking into a fishing boat
- Didn't you hear us, we said it CAN'T go over land. OH GOD! NO, LOOK OUT ...

When planning your next trip, don't forget to travel by ekranoplan, the entirely water-based way of going by plane without ever getting more than a few feet above the ground and then forgetting about that and accidentally zooming up a beach and ploughing through someone's house again.

'Oh my God, we're heading for the beach'

'I'm sorry, I don't speak English'

FOCUS ON FRANCE

**OTHER BITS
OF WESTERN
EUROPE**
GERMANY, AUSTRIA,
SWITZERLAND, ALL OVER HERE

FRANCE
WHERE FRENCH
PEOPLE LIVE

**SPAIN 'N'
PORTUGAL**
DON'T LIKE TO BE REFERRED
TO LIKE THIS

AFRICA
BUT ONLY THE VERY TOP BIT

a.k.a.

RÉPUBLIQUE FRANÇAISE

France legalised same-sex marriage in 2013. At the same time they also legalised same-sex affairs.

Population:

67 MILLION

The Louvre is one of the most visited museums in the world and is full of visitors from many different nations, all saying 'Ooh, isn't it smaller than it looks in pictures?'

Capital:

PARIS

Under French law, 40 per cent of all music played on radio stations must be of French origin. As a consequence, everyone in France is sick of 'Joe le taxi'.

The French and the British have co-operated on many major transport projects including Concorde, the Channel Tunnel and of course the Talbot Samba.

Currency:

EURO

Although the French work hard to preserve the integrity and traditions of the French language, many modern words are the same as English, such as 'l'internet', 'un blog', 'un email' and 'le wifi' or, as British people trying to use a French keyboard would have it, 'le zifi ... arrrgh, why is the Z up there?'

Famous people:

GÉRARD DEPARDIEU, BRIGITTE BARDOT, ZINEDINE ZIDANE, ERIC CANTONA, THIERRY HENRY, NAPOLEON BONAPARTE

France produces almost 1 billion tons of cheese a year. And then makes a little more for export.

BEHIND THE SCENES

The presenters decided to prove that old Maseratis are brilliant, with a bloody-minded trip to France. This was only the second thing ever filmed for *The Grand Tour*. And the night before shooting, James broke his arm like a big clot.

Above, James attends to the engine of his Maserati with the help of an unruly ape.

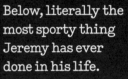

Above, the man who did an *homage* to a 1980s Volkswagen advert, just as the smart money moved out.

Below, literally the most sporty thing Jeremy has ever done in his life.

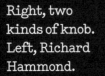

Right, two kinds of knob. Left, Richard Hammond.

James broke his arm by falling in the street after a night in the pub. He swore that these were completely unrelated facts.

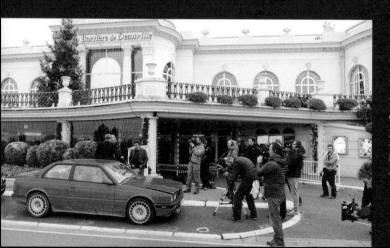

Count the cameras. There are usually three on a 'Big Three' presenter shoot like this.

Above, a beached
buffoon in an old
Italian car.

Above, bang on cue, the
official *Grand Tour* boot
licker shows up.

Below, a *Grand Tour* favourite:
the 'describe-a-fish' game.

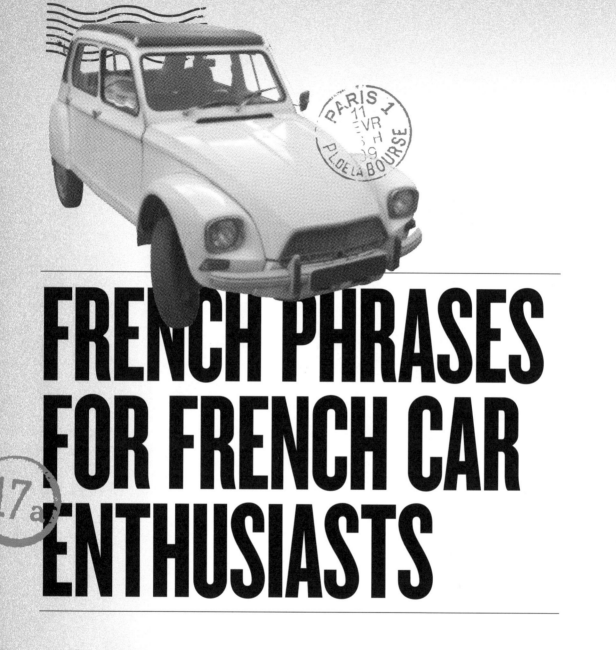

FRENCH PHRASES FOR FRENCH CAR ENTHUSIASTS

If you're a French car enthusiast in Britain you'll probably want to take your car for a driving holiday in its homeland of France. Here are some phrases to help you on your way.

I'm sorry, I seem to have suffered lift-off oversteer into your field.
Je suis désolé, il me semble avoir souffert lift-off survirage dans votre champ.

Excuse me if the appearance of my Peugeot 3008 is what caused your wife's nausea.
Excusez-moi si l'apparition de ma Peugeot 3008 est causé ce la nausée de votre femme.

This part seems to have come off in my hand.
Cette partie semble avoir comme dans ma main.

I could not hear my sat-nav over all the rattling and that is why I drove into your river.
Je ne pouvais pas entendre sur toute la crécelle mon sat-nav et voilà pourquoi je suis entré dans votre rivière.

This other part seems to have come off in my hand.
Semble avoir cette autre partie que dans ma main.

I did not realise the name Renault Fuego was so literal.
Je ne savais pas le nom Renault Fuego était si littérale.

Please do not touch that, it is made of extremely thin plastic.
S'il vous plaît ne touchez pas que, il est fait de plastique extrêmement mince.

The damage was caused by a mouse that accessed the interior through one of the panel gaps.
Les dégâts ont été causés par une souris qui accède à l'intérieur par l'un des panneau lacunes.

Another part has come off in my hand and unfortunately it is the steering wheel.
Une autre partie est venu dans ma main et, malheureusement, il est le volant.

Do you have another Saxo, mine seems to have gone soggy?
Avez-vous une autre Saxo, le mien semble avoir été détrempée?

POSTCARD

FROM THE TENT

Here we are beside beautiful Loch Ness, which is in Scotland. We're staying in a massive old building which might have been a boarding school or an asylum, we're not sure. With the *Grand Tour* team in residence it feels like both. Place is so big James went wandering around the central quad the other night and then couldn't remember how to get back to his room. Fortunately, we could all remember the way to the local pub so we went there. That's the best thing to do in this part of the world. Admire beautiful view, then go to local pub. And repeat. Except when we have to make a show. Which we did. And it went very well. So the next day we did another one. Two reasons for this; first, Richard and James are genuinely obsessed with seeing the Loch Ness

monster and Jeremy is genuinely obsessed with proving that it doesn't exist. Second, we like it here and it saves moving the tent and finding somewhere else to put it. So we've filmed two episodes. And now we're off to the local pub again. Bye,

THE GRAND TOUR

THE CELEBRITY
BRAIN CRASH
machine

Owners' Instruction Manual

The Celebrity Brain Crash machine was one of the highlights of the first series of *The Grand Tour*, especially among people who didn't actually watch the first series of *The Grand Tour*. However, due to a series of technical problems out of our control – e.g. celebrities dying – we didn't actually get to see the machine in action, and this left some people wondering, what is it all about? Well, the Celebrity Brain Crash machine was created by some of the world's top scientists and James May's friend Ken, and it's inspired by the actual tests used by the Royal Air Force to ruthlessly weed out weaker candidates during the selection process to work in their canteen. But how, you might be wondering, does the machine actually work? Well, to give you a flavour of its highly complex inner workings, here is the official start-up procedure that must be used to enter the world of Celebrity Brain Crash. Cue the absolutely terrible introductory graphics ...

1. Open the construm valves
(front and rear).

2. Using the Bellingham gauge on the front, wait until the forstal pressure has reached at least 2.2 (Gna).

3. Once the correct pressure is achieved, de-gas the glorring facet by depressing the obviation nozzle cap and turning it ambi-clockwise.

4. Wait until the high-pitched noise has ceased and then press the ignition spockler **NO MORE** than 18 times.

5. A red light will illuminate to confirm that both Kestrel hammers have engaged and the antion rachet is now active. At this point carefully apply pressure to the tweest cap.

6. Check that both Hampson valves are in the upward position and fully de-knuckled.

7. You may now depress the capital hat to start the master processor.

8. Upon start-up, the main screen should show the Swannage prompt for approximately 37 minutes after which it will ask, **'Do you want to initiate contra mass protocol (Y/N)?'** DO NOT press Y or N.

9. Press the hat symbol button for 3–19 seconds (depending on temperature) until you see a red dot on the screen. Do not look directly at the dot for longer than necessary.

10. A loud beep indicates that the master **RIM** head is now in place and you must proceed with the anterior start-up procedure within 2 seconds or the transfer caps will become friberated.

11. The Anson capsule will now issue a secondary code prompt (aural, visual and the other one). When received, immediately enter your **PIN** into the lower handset.

12. The initiation tone will sound and the main lightbar should cycle through the standardised emergency protocols. **Do not be alarmed**, this is not the sign that there is a fire, unless you smell burning, in which case it is.

13. When all seven of the green LEDs have fallen off, you may hold down the **RETURN** key, the **SPACE** bar and the **LOOKS A BIT LIKE A CAT** button to authorise the Jepson scripts to initialise (two per sealed Lang unit).

14. Since the previous step can take up to nine (minutes or hours, latitude dependent), use this opportunity to inspect the mole heads for tears and other signs of damage. Rinse out as necessary.

⚠ **WARNING**, the next few steps are not for the faint-hearted.

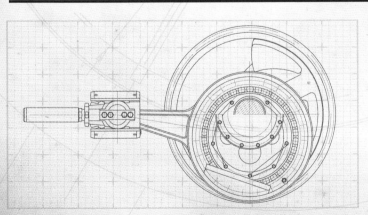

15. When the omnivium clasp opens, the main switch bank is ready to be depressurised. Doing so will tell the key batch hangers to power across. This will happen sequentially and may be accompanied by a low smell. Do not be alarmed more than is normal.

16. Open the vents on the Anders-Gnilling unit as required.

17. Initiate a primary load bank processor cache test by scrolling through the on-screen menu until you find the option marked 'Optimal confragration routine'.

18. Once the multi core **B90-4** chips have reached full interfaciality (as indicated by the masterboard control panel turning green or something similar), you may enter the kerl prompt (**A or B**) to trigger an internal clock sequence to initiate the game software.

19. When the Janet flash becomes white, the on-screen prompt will ask if you wish to load full protocols (**Ooh, yes please / No thank you, but thanks for asking**). Select the first option using the direction-control helm. Be warned, it may be quite hot and also sticky.

20. When you see the full welcome screen, take a note of the numbers displayed on the ulterior display bulb and do not show them to anyone else, even if they ask.

21. Activate the test cycle for the playing interface control league by flicking the far left Massingham switch to the often position.

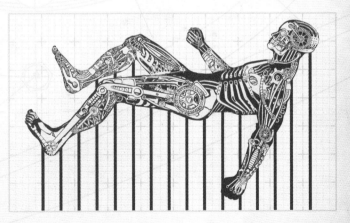

22. When the blue light goes out, you can twist the Greasby slot to the ... actually, forget it, the celebrity has just died. Again.

23. Please now turn the machine OFF and allow it to cool down.

CLARKSON & HAMMOND'S WORD SEARCH

J	A	M	E	S	I	S	A	B	E	L	L	E	N	N
A	G	R	U	L	W	T	A	B	E	Y	U	C	V	
M	A	Y	S	M	E	L	L	S	P	K	G	N	A	
E	E	F	L	K	A	E	Q	Y	P	J	K	S	G	
S	A	H	J	A	M	E	S	I	S	A	T	W	A	
I	B	N	W	A	Y	W	I	S	H	R	U	J	D	
S	Q	T	U	T	M	Y	I	O	F	J	F	H	A	
A	R	K	W	E	S	E	B	N	M	X	C	B	A	
W	J	A	M	E	S	I	S	A	N	I	P	P	L	
A	C	B	U	E	G	D	H	I	A	J	D	V	N	
Z	C	B	J	A	M	E	S	I	S	A	K	N	O	
Z	B	E	C	T	H	W	U	I	A	A	N	D	G	
O	L	E	J	W	D	H	D	H	T	Y	T	B	C	
C	F	A	J	A	M	E	S	I	S	A	N	I	D	

JEREMY CLARKSON'S

SPOT THE DIFFERENCE

JAMES MAY'S

MATCH THE STAR TO THE CAR

Certain top celebrity faces are forever associated with a certain car, but can you match the stars below to the machine that everyone always mentions in relation to their name?

RICHARD HAMMOND'S FIENDISHLY DIFFICULT INTERNATIONAL QUIZ

1. The Austrian city of Vienna is the capital of which country?

2. Which country does Air India come from?

3. In which country would you find the German region of Bavaria?

4. The Arc de Triomphe is a French monument located in which country?

5. Which country's national anthem is called 'O Canada'?

6. Name the country at the very South of Africa.

7. Australian racing driver Mark Webber is from which country?

8. Which country is someone from if they tell you they are 'Japanese'?

9. Ferraris come from which Italian country?

10. Which country does Chinese food come from?

WITTER
IS
COMING

JEREMIE
OF HOUSE
CLARKSON

THE CLASH OF THE IDIOTS

GRAND
OF TOURS

YOU
TOUR
OR
YOU DIE

RICHYRD
OF HOUSE HAMMOND

JAYMES
OF HOUSE MAY

SERIES 2

THE TOUR CONTINUES...

SERIES

2

DUBAI

HAMMOND
GOES MAD
WITH A
TINY TANK
IN DUBAI.

DUBAI

THE LITTLE TANK IS CALLED A
RIPSAW. ALTHOUGH IT WEIGHS
OVER FOUR TONNES, IT CAN PASS
OVER ANY TERRAIN WITHOUT
LEAVING A MARK, AS RICHARD
DEMONSTRATES HERE.

MOZAMBIQUE

'A MERCY
MISSION
TO FEED
THE NEEDY.
PUT BONO
ON SPEED
DIAL.'

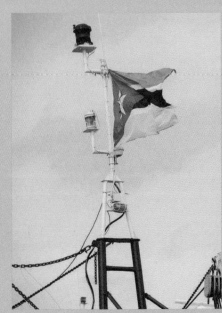

SERIES

2

CROATIA

'THREE MEN, NO PLAN. CONFUSION AND CHAOS RESULTS.'

SERIES

2

SWITZERLAND

'PAST, PRESENT AND FUTURE SUPERCARS BATTLE IT OUT IN THE MOUNTAINS.'

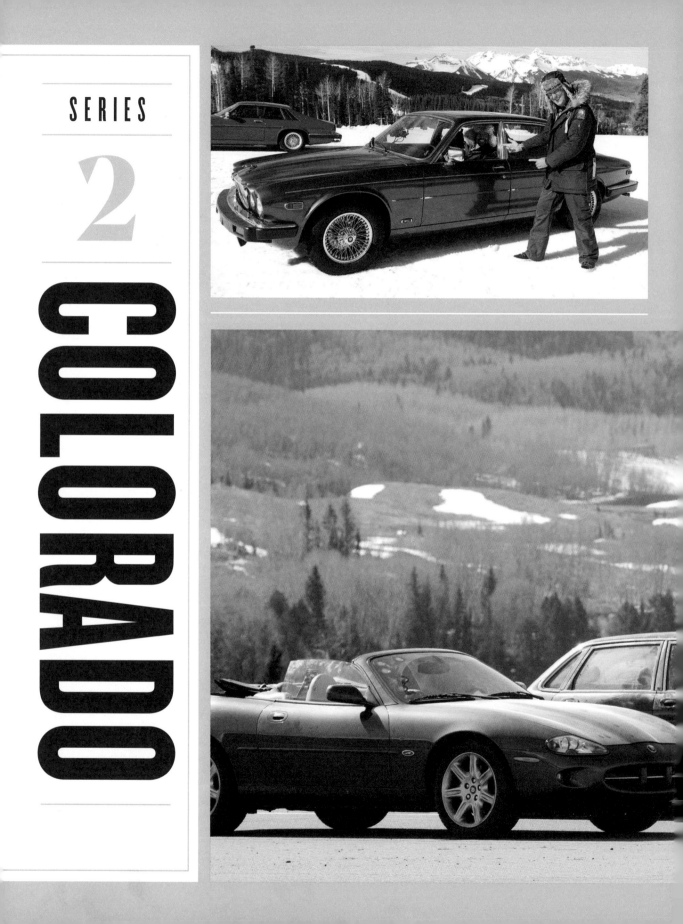

SERIES

2

COLORADO

'AN
AMERICAN
ROAD TRIP
TO
DEMONSTRATE
THE GENIUS
OF OLD
JAAAAGS.'

INDEX

PICTURE CREDITS

All images © Shutterstock.com with the following exceptions: Andrew Harker/Alamy Stock Photo p251 (Red Reliant Scimitar GTE 2 door coupé); Action Plus Sports Images/Alamy Stock Photo p137 (Hovercraft); Adrian Sherratt/Alamy Stock Photo p192 (Swindon Roundabout); Braniff International Airlines pp 150–151 (1970s passenger plane interior); Danny Martindale/WireImage/Getty Images p79 (Katie Price); David Howells/Corbis via Getty Images p79 (Jordan Belfort); David Thorpe/Alamy Stock Photo p251 (Abandoned decaying Reliant Scimitar); David Warner Ellis/Redferns/Getty Images p179 (Golden Earring); Dennis Chamberlin/The Denver Post via Getty Images p137 (Maserati Biturbo); Ellis O'Brien/© Amazon Prime Video pp 10, 12–13, 14–15, 18–19, 20–21, 26–27, 38–39, 62, 64–65, 69, 70–71, 74–75, 76–77, 80–81, 82–83, 85, 88, 90–91, 94–95, 96–97, 104–105, 106, 112, 114, 119, 120–121, 124–125, 126–127, 130–131, 134, 136, 138, 140–141, 144–145, 146–147, 148–149, 154–155, 157 (top), 160–161, 164–165, 166–167, 170–171, 172–173, 175, 177, 182–183, 186–187, 200–201, 202–203, 204–205, 208–209, 216–217, 220–221, 223, 224–225, 226, 228–229, 232–233, 234–235, 240–241, 253, 254–255, 256–257, 258–259, 260–261, 262–263, 264–265, 266–267, 272; Ethan Miller/Getty Images p79 (Jordan Knight); Everett Collection Inc/Alamy Stock Photo p41 (Evel Knievel & Sue Lyon); Goddard on the Go/Alamy Stock Photo p135 (Alfa Romeo 4C); H Armstrong Roberts/Classic Stock/Getty Images p152 (Two 1960s businessmen); H Armstrong Roberts/Classic Stock/Getty Images p153 (Air stewardess serving drinks); Heritage Image Partnership Ltd/Alamy Stock Photo p153 (Passengers boarding a Britannia Airways plane); IsKa/Alamy Stock Photo p86 (Volvo V70); James Dimmock/© Amazon Prime Video pp 6–7, 28, 100, 196; Jeremy Fletcher/Getty Images p250 (Princess Anne at Horse Trials with members of the Royal Canadian Mounted Police, 1968); Jordan Gast/Alamy Stock Photo p135 (Dodge Challenger Hellcat); Josh Lefkowitz/Getty Images p79 (Jordan Clarkson); Justin Setterfield/Stringer/Getty Images p179 (Sir Chris Hoy); Keystone Pictures USA/Alamy Stock Photo p40 (Evel Knievel); Liam Richardson/Alamy Stock Photo p132 (Vauxhall Astra Diesel); Mark Thompson/Getty Images p79 (Eddie Jordan); Martin Berry/Alamy Stock Photo p108 (Holden Commodore SS); MHA Archive/Alamy Stock Photo p193 (Old Greek Renault postal service van); National Motor Museum/Heritage Images/Getty Images p55 (1957 Mercedes Benz 300 SL Gullwing); Newzulu/Alamy Stock Photo p179 (Simon Pegg); Nick Veasey/Getty Images p110 (X-ray of human hands on steering wheel); Nick Veasey/Getty Images p111 (X-ray of human seated at steering wheel); Noam Galai/Getty Images p79 (Jordin Sparks); Noel Yates/Alamy Stock Photo p176 (1970s roadside camping with Ford Cortina); Pascal Parrot/Sygma via Getty Images pp 218–219 (Ari Vatanen); Paul Heinrich/Alamy Stock Photo p251 (Yellow Reliant Scimitar sports car); Paul Natkin/Wire Image/Getty Images p179 (Brian Johnson); PBP Galleries/Alamy Stock Photo p251 (1976 Reliant Scimitar GTE SE 6, CSCC Future Classic race, Snetterton, Norfolk, UK); PCN Photography/Alamy Stock Photo p79 (Michael Jordan); Peter Parks/AFP/Getty Images p57 (Advertisement for the Roewe 750 car); Pictorial Press Ltd/Alamy Stock Photo p179 (Nena); Ray Bellisario/Popperfoto/Getty Images p250 (Princess Anne opening the Dexter Paper Mill at Chirnside, Scotland, 1973); Ray Bellisario/Popperfoto/Getty Images p250 (Princess Anne riding during an Inter-Schools gymkhana at Moat House Farm in Benenden, Kent, 1967); Richard Porter pp 37, 63, 200–201, 223, 238–239; Richard Sheppard/Alamy Stock Photo p251 (Old Reliant Scimitar in need of restoration); Ron Galella/WireImage/Getty Images p250 (Princess Anne at the Wyle Horse Trials, 1976); SFM Archivio Storico/Alamy Stock Photo p214 (Man in swimming trunks); SJAdvertArchive/Alamy Stock Photo p152 (Serving drinks, KLM Airlines); Sjo/Getty Images p66 (Porsche 911 Targa Netherlands police car); Stuart Pettican/© Amazon Prime Video pp 8–9, 248–249; Studiomode/Alamy Stock Photo p79 (Jordans cereal boxes); Tass via Getty Images p227 (KM Ekranoplan); Thomas Samson/AFP/Getty Images p133 (Renault Megane RS); Tim Graham/Getty Images p250 (Princess Anne walking her dogs, 1974); Tim Graham/Getty Images p250 (Princess Anne in Barbour coat and hat at the Windsor Horse Trials, 1983); Tom Kelley Archive/Getty Images p50 (Travel agent on phone); United Archives GmbH/Alamy Stock Photo p174 (Still from *Carry On Camping*); William Arthur/Alamy Stock Photo p251 (Metallic Green Reliant Scimitar GTE SE6a model 1981).

While every effort has been made to trace the owners of copyright material reproduced herein and secure permissions, the publishers would like to apologise for any omissions and will be pleased to incorporate missing acknowledgements in any future edition of this book.

←CT→Corrections and Mistakes

Due to a number of errors that we're going to blame on the most junior member of the team, this book contains the below mistakes for which we can only apologgise.

Page 14 – List of countries in which you must drive on the left accidentally includes the word 'Germany'.

Page 19 – List of traditional food stuffs should not include the word 'pebbles'.

Page 34 – The correct name is 'London Heathrow Airport' and not, as written, 'London Hammond Idiotport'.

Page 38 – Most of these are wrong, especially the one about trombones.

Page 45 – Complaints should actually be addressed to Pip Glisby, unless too large to fit through the letter-hole.

Page 47 – Section on sun cream accidentally contains the phrase 'makes a delicious accompaniment to fish, chicken and salads'. Please ignore the word 'salads'.

Page 51 – Contrary to the advice on this page, when meeting King Felipe VI of Spain it is not protocol to shout 'HOOPLA!' in his face.

Page 53 – Sentence that ends 'and is extremely poisonous' wrongly contains the word 'not'.

Page 65 – There is no such place as 'James May International Mayport'.

Page 68 – Contrary to the claim, airlines do not give out free upgrades to anyone who checks in with the phrase 'Don't you know who I am?'

Page 70 – Where written 'Generally Claxon' it should of course say 'Jeremy Claxon'.

Page 72 – He isn't called 'Richard Hammered'.

Page 78 – There is no such word as 'meatgasm', especially not in this context.

Page 88 – Last line of third paragraph should say 'take in the stunning views', not, as written, 'and then repeatedly bludgeon the bag'.

Page 90 – Picture shows James May and not, as printed, 'the famous piles of rotting meat'.

Page 101 – Do not Google any of this stuff.

Page 111 – This is not Jeremy Clarkson's real face. Or leg.

Page 119 – Picture shows the famous piles of rotting meat and not, as printed, 'James May'.

Page 131 – This did not happen.

Page 132 – This definitely did not happen.

Page 147 – List entitled 'Seven things you really should try adding lemon juice to' accidentally includes the words 'your eyes'.

Page 156 – Richard Hammond has never even met Beyoncé.

Page 166 – Section on etiquette wrongly contains the words, 'Floor it, your majesty'.

Page 180 – List should not include Hootie and The Blowfish, for obvious reasons.

Page 201 – Section on Dutch footballers should not include Vas Deferens.

Page 220 – Don't tell anyone about any of this.

Page 309 – Page does not exist.